Research

and

Composition

A Guide for the Beginning Researcher

JOYCE INGLISH

JOAN E. JACKSON

Mesa Community College

PRENTICE-HALL, INC., Englewood Cliffs, N.J. 07632

Library of Congress Cataloging in Publication Data

INGLISH, JOYCE, (date)
  Research and composition.

  1. Research. 2. Report writing. I. JACKSON,
JOAN E., (date) joint author. II. Title.
LB2369.I48   808'.023   76–54259

Printed in the United States of America
10 9 8 7 6 5 4

PRENTICE-HALL INTERNATIONAL, INC., *London*
PRENTICE-HALL OF AUSTRALIA PTY. LIMITED, *Sydney*
PRENTICE-HALL OF CANADA, LTD., *Toronto*
PRENTICE-HALL OF INDIA PRIVATE LIMITED, *New Delhi*
PRENTICE-HALL OF JAPAN, INC., *Tokyo*
PRENTICE-HALL OF SOUTHEAST ASIA PTE. LTD., *Singapore*
WHITEHALL BOOKS LIMITED, *Wellington, New Zealand*

Contents

PRACTICE

TYPING

EVALUATION

Foreword

This manual is a product of the classroom experiences of two English professors who take pride in their teaching at an open-door college. They believe that their students are truly valuable to our world but need to learn how to contribute clearly and positively to its improvement through their skills and knowledge.

The manual is not a guide for the advanced stylist; neither is it an elementary introduction to writing organized papers. It is a combination of creative assignments for locating information through reading and presenting it in planned papers suitable to most courses. The ideas for research are individually provocative and will stimulate student curiosity. The formats of the reports are skillfully developed through sequential assignments. They have been classroom tested; they work well.

More importantly, students who have used the manual like it. They endorse it as a successful guide to writing library papers. I respect their evaluation.

WALT HODGES, Chairman
English Department
Mesa Community College

Preface

A wise professor once said: "Teachers, realizing how much there is to know and how many years they have labored to learn but a small portion of that knowledge, want to share all they have acquired with their students. Often the students, overwhelmed by the bulk of instructional materials and the length and complexity of assignments, become frustrated and either give up or resign themselves to failure." His advice to teachers was, "In the few weeks you have with a student, don't try to teach too much, and what you do teach, teach well."

Traditionally, textbooks have emphasized scholarly research without regard for the fact that beginning research students are seldom equipped with necessary library or composition skills. These students need opportunities to produce excellent papers, not ten years from now when they are working on a college master's thesis, but now. In an era when educators complain that students read less, think less, and write not at all, mediocrity has become acceptable. Through the combination of carefully selected, high-interest topics and a gradual introduction to research tools and skills, students can realize competence, even excellence.

To the Student

Research and Composition is an attempt to provide you with the writing skills that will serve you long after your formal education is completed. This is no small matter in a world where many of the skills learned in school are obsolete before graduation. We do not foresee good writing becoming obsolete, however. Indeed, it may be one of the few marketable skills remaining five years after your graduation.

This manual contains not only the explanations of research techniques, but assignments as well. We hope you will read it, write in it, and make it your personal handbook. Samples of students' writing are included throughout. These samples should encourage you to believe that you too can produce clear, readable, and excellent papers.

ACKNOWLEDGMENTS

The authors gratefully acknowledge the contributions of the following people in the preparation of this book: Sharon Kuntz for her sunny disposition and invaluable work in arranging format and typing the manuscript; Debbie Hunkler for typing and proofreading; our friend and colleague, Walter Hodges, for his support through all stages of this work.

We thank the following reviewers for their careful reading of and intelligent suggestions for improving our manuscript: Professor Ann C. Briegal, DeKalb College, Clarkston, Georgia; Professor Kim Flachman, Department of English, California State College at Bakersfield; Professor James M. Williams, Director of Communications, Johnson County Community College, Overland Park, Kansas; Professor Peter T. Zoller, Department of English, Wichita State University, Wichita, Kansas; Professor C. Jeriel Howard, Dallas, Texas; Professor G. Dale Gleason, Hutchinson Community Jr. College, Hutchinson, Kansas.

Most of all, we thank our students at Mesa Community College whose genuine desire for quality instruction inspired us to write this book and whose honest efforts to produce excellent papers provided us with the samples reproduced herein.

I. J. INGLISH, Ph.D.
J. E. JACKSON, M.S.

Getting Started

What Is Research?

If you have ever found yourself in the middle of a friendly dis-
agreement with a friend or relative, you may know the feeling that
comes with a need to prove that you are right on even the most trivial
subject:

Who ran the first four-minute mile?
What play had the longest Broadway run?
What is believed to be the origin of the Egyptian pyramids?
Who slew Medusa?
Where did Great Aunt Matilda get her fortune?

Frequently, these trivial disputes send you to the nearest encyclopedia,
The Guinness Book of World Records, or your Uncle Harry, the family
expert on trivia. Some are so haunted that they write to "Dear Abby" or
"Answer Line" and wait months or even longer for a reply. Others will
run to the nearest library and with the help of a reference librarian seek
the proper volume for an answer.

At times finding the answer becomes secondary to an earnest quest
to learn more. You read until, much to your surprise, you find that it's
time for the library to close. What an exhilarating experience that is,
to lose yourself in a search for knowledge! All else fades from the mind
as the desire to know takes over. And that is research—the honest desire
to know something, coupled with an energetic search to find the answer.
Occasionally, the learning is followed by a sense of urgency to write
down what you have learned so that others might share the knowledge.

Research should be an honest desire to explore, observe, or analyze
a subject. On occasion it may even take the form of creating. Its reward

should be the satisfaction that comes with knowing. If it does not meet either of these requirements, students will think of research as nothing more than a drab chore. Students, of course, do not always experience this feeling of satisfaction. They do not always feel inspired. Why then should they pursue research? Perhaps the only answer is that much of education consists by necessity of simulated experiences. Undoubtedly, the college student will have to demonstrate growth in subject areas many times over through research papers. Consequently, training in research cannot be ignored. It may be helpful if the teacher strives to supply the student with:

1. A choice of thought-provoking subjects designed to stimulate interest and imagination.

2. Skills to locate appropriate materials for solving problems.

3. A desire to write or record in a paper what has been learned.

If the student will contribute his activity and cooperative participation, beginning research can be a profitable learning experience and perhaps an enjoyable one as well. A student need not travel far to find a subject for research. He can simply begin with himself.

The question "Who am I?" has haunted man. Despite his struggles through the centuries to build empires and construct civilizations, he has never been able to answer collectively, "I am Babylon, I am Rome, I am Athens." Nor has he been satisfied with, "I am a cathedral, I am a pyramid, I am a skyscraper." He, like Tennyson's Ulysses, might say, "I am part of all that I have met." He might realize, as did John Donne, that "No man is an island, entire of itself; every man is a piece of the continent, a part of the main." Satirically, he might write of himself as did E. B. White in "About Myself"[1]:

> I am a man of medium height. I keep my records in a Weis Folder Re-order Number 8003. The unpaid balance of my estimated tax for the year 1945 is item 3 less the sum of items 4 and 5. My eyes are gray. . . .
> I was born in District Number 5903, New York State. My birth is registered in Volume 3/58 of the Department of Health. My father was a man of medium height. His telephone number was 484. My mother was a housewife. Her eyes were blue. Neither parent had a social security number and neither was secure socially. They drove to the depot behind an unnumbered horse.

Or poetically he might assess himself as did Wallace Stevens in "I Measure Myself"[2]:

---

[1] From E. B. White, "About Myself." Reprinted by permission of Harper & Row Publishers.

[2] From "Six Significant Landscapes," Part III, *The Collected Poems of Wallace Stevens.* Copyright © 1954 by Alfred A. Knopf, Inc. Reprinted by permission.

I measure myself
Against a tall tree.
I find that I am much taller,
For I reach right up to the sun,
With my eye;
And I reach to the shore of the sea
With my ear.
Nevertheless, I dislike
The way the ants crawl
In and out of my shadow.

All of us have stood with Alice and looked at a Caterpillar sitting on a mushroom and smoking a hookah. The Caterpillar sleepily asks, "Who are *you?*" With Alice we have answered, "I–I hardly know, Sir, just at present. . . ." The beginning of a semester, like Wonderland, is a chaotic, topsy-turvy time. Indeed, you may be wondering who you are, why on earth you let yourself in for all this bother, and how, knowing as little as you do, you can possibly write a research paper. Alice eventually got herself back to the right size and remembered that she was Alice, so there is hope for you. Besides, you already know more than you think you do—about yourself and about research.

Answer as many of the following personal data questions as you can from your own knowledge; for those that you cannot answer right now, determine the quickest and most reliable source of information, and you will have taken the first step toward research. An *authority* is one who can supply reliable knowledge. *Other* might be a family *Bible,* genealogical chart, grade report, etc.

> Knowledge is of two kinds: we know a subject ourselves, or we know where we can find information upon it.
>
> Boswell's *Life of Johnson* (1775)

Who Am I?

Personal Data:

	Self	Authority	Legal Medical Document	Other
1. My name is _____				
2. My father's name is _____				
My mother's name is _____				
My father was born in _____ (*year*)				
_____ (*location*)				

	SELF	AUTHORITY	LEGAL MEDICAL DOCUMENT	OTHER

My mother was born in _____
(*year*)

_____
(*location*)

My brothers are _____

_____

My sisters are _____

_____

3. My grandparents (*mother's side*) are

_____

My grandparents (*father's side*) are

_____

_____

They came from (*mother's side*) _____

_____

(*father's side*) _____

_____

4. My wife/husband is _____

My children are _____

_____

_____

5. I live at (*address*) _____

_____

My telephone number is _____

	SELF	AUTHORITY	LEGAL MEDICAL DOCUMENT	OTHER

6. I was born:

   City and state _____

   Hospital _____

   Attending physician _____

   Date _____

7. My social security number is _____

   _____

   My driver's license number is _____

   _____

   My car license number is _____

   _____

8. My blood type is _____

   My height is _____

   My weight is _____

   My hair color is _____

   My eye color is _____

9. I went to elementary school (*name of school, location, teacher's name*)

   First grade _____

   _____

   Second grade _____

   _____

	SELF	AUTHORITY	LEGAL MEDICAL DOCUMENT	OTHER
Third grade _____				
_____				
Fourth grade _____				
_____				
Fifth grade _____				
_____				
Sixth grade _____				
_____				
Seventh grade _____				
_____				
Eighth grade _____				
_____				
My favorite subjects were _____				
_____				
10. I went to high school (*name of school, city, state*) _____				
_____				
I was graduated from (*name of school, date*) _____				
My favorite subjects were _____				
_____				

	SELF	AUTHORITY	LEGAL MEDICAL DOCUMENT	OTHER
My favorite extracurricular activities were _____				
11. I have attended college (*name of school or schools, location*) _____ _____ _____				
My major is _____				
12. I have been employed at (*names of employers, jobs held*) _____ _____ _____				
13. I was in the service (*branch, when, where, ranks held*) _____ _____				
14. During my life I have received recognition for _____ _____				
15. I like (*list as many as you wish: foods, books, classes, people, hobbies, etc.*) ____ _____ _____ _____				

	SELF	AUTHORITY	LEGAL MEDICAL DOCUMENT	OTHER
I dislike (*list as many as you wish*) _____				
16. Three people knowledgeable about my background, character, and abilities are:				

Research on yourself is used most frequently in furnishing informa-   **EXERCISE I**
tion to colleges or for job applications. Using the material you have
assembled, arrange certain portions of it into a personal data sheet.
Whenever you write to a prospective employer, you should enclose one with your letter of application.

The data sheet (resumé) conveniently puts all pertinent information in one place where it can be scanned quickly. It allows you to
state your experiences and qualifications without the appearance of
boasting. While not every employer will be interested in all of the
information you give, each can select what he regards as vital. Study
Figure 1 on page 10 as a guide for setting up your own data sheet.

1. Using the information you have recorded under the Self column   **EXERCISE II**
of Who Am I, write a well-developed paragraph from a first-person
point of view. (First person is either *I* or *we*.)

    Much of what we know about ourselves develops bit by bit
through the years. As we learn to walk, talk, dress ourselves, love our
families, play with our brothers and sisters, go to school, and acquire likes and dislikes, each of us forms a creature called I. Each I
speaks with a unique voice. My name is Karen Ann Collins. My
father's parents, Bert J. and Virginia Collins, grew up and were married in Pennsylvania, where my father was born. My maternal grandparents, Henry and Helen Dill, were raised and married in New
Jersey, but moved to Cleveland, Ohio, where mother was born. My
parents, Edwin J. Collins and Virginia Dill Collins, moved to Mesa,
Arizona, where I was born on 11 December 1957, in Southside District Hospital. My four brothers, two sisters, parents, and I now live
at 3096 South Ashburn Street, Tempe, Arizona. I attended Our Lady

                                        578 W. Parkway Ave.
                                        Phoenix, AZ 85404
                                        254-4598

                          DATA SHEET

                        Tracy Jackson

Place and date of birth: El Paso, Texas   6 February 1958

Height: 5' 7 3/4"

Weight: 130 lbs.

Health: Excellent

Sex: Female

Education: Graduated from McClintock High School, Tempe, Arizona, 1975
               Now attending Mesa Community College, Mesa, Arizona
               Major: Pre-med

High School Activities: Member student council
                           Editor high school newspaper
                           Participated as actor and stagehand in plays
                           Played flute in high school band

College Activities: Freshman class president
                     Member Associated Student Governing Board
                     Played flute in MCC Marching Band

Honors Earned: Outstanding journalism student - McClintock High School
                Girls' State Representative
                Art award for original needlework design

Job Experience: YWCA camp counselor, 1973
                 Volunteer work with retarded children helping to
                 develop social, personal, and educational skills
                 Volunteer recreation leader for Tempe Parks and
                 Recreation Program working with elementary children
                 with games, arts, and crafts
                 MCC Campus Publicity Office doing art layouts

References: The following people have offered to furnish references
             for me:

             Ms. Carol Eichelberger, Nutritionist, Arizona State Health
             Department, Phoenix, Arizona.

             Dr. J. Reuben Sheeler, Minister, St. Paul African Methodist
             Episcopal Church, Houston, Texas.

             Mr. Ed Lewis, Publisher, _Essence_ magazine, New York City,
             New York.

Fig. 1. Data Sheet.

of Mount Carmel Grade School for eight years, was graduated from McClintock High School, and received an Art Scholarship of $150. I am now a Freshman at Mesa Community College, majoring in fashion merchandising and minoring in art. To earn money for school expenses, I work at the Regal Fork Buffet, as a waitress. Here I pause, realizing how little one paragraph can tell of the triumphs and heartaches of eighteen years.

2. Using the information recorded under the columns marked Legal, Medical Document, or Other Documents, write a well-developed paragraph from a third-person point of view. (Third person uses the given name or the he/she pronouns.) Cite sources for the information.

As the world's population increases, numbers and documents play an expanding role in each person's life. The individual, ushered into the world accompanied by a birth certificate, departs, his death carefully recorded and filed. In between these events, he receives dozens of licenses, certificates, and cards—all painstakingly numbered. According to his birth certificate, Michael John Curtis was born in Cambridge, England, at South Hill Maternity Hospital, on 3 February 1955. The attending physician was Dr. Steven Easton. Curtis' health card lists his blood type O-RH positive. After emigrating to the United States, he acquired a social security card, number 519–11–6230, from the Department of Health, Education, and Welfare. The Drivers' License Bureau in Phoenix, Arizona, issued him a driver's license, number CO36721, after he had successfully completed written and driving requirements. His 1974 Ford Torino bears license number CXT–391. The city of Mesa, Arizona, numbers his home 654 West El Camino Drive, and the telephone company extends him the courtesy of a phone, number 832-5908. He does not try to remember all of these numbers, for he conveniently has his cards filed in Index 714.

For your personal data sheet and two paragraphs, you have cited research information stored in your mind, secured from family, relatives, or friends, and entered on medical, legal, and other documents. In recording this information, you have relied on techniques essential for all sound research composition:

1. All names, dates, places, and numbers must be exact. Names of persons and places must be spelled correctly; days, months, years must be written precisely as given; numbers must be accurately transcribed. Readers are entitled to reliable, valid, and accurate information.

2. Sources must be identified for your reader. First-person point of view establishes *I* as the origin of the source, unless *I* states otherwise. The more formal third-person point of view requires identification of persons or printed material supplying the information. This acknowledgement may be made in the text—e.g., your second paragraph—or as footnotes.

3. To communicate with your reader, you must be clear, presenting information in a form he understands. In your personal data sheet, the

labels identified the different areas; in your paragraphs, standard sentence patterns enabled your reader to follow your ideas as they developed.

The paper "Help for the Child Abuser," which begins on page 101, demonstrates how one student incorporated exactness, clarity, and citing of sources in her composition. The paper also illustrates a number of elements essential to the formation of a readable, accurate, organized, and developed research paper. As you read, observe that the student needed skills in specific areas to achieve the finished paper. Consider these skills carefully. You, too, need them before you write.

SKILL IN THIS AREA	RESULTS IN
Library	Knowing how to use the library to select and locate materials needed in the research paper.
Reading, sorting, and note-taking	Knowing how to extract information from sources and how to record and file that information for easy, orderly use when writing the paper.
Documentation	Knowing how to identify and utilize the specialized tools for research that give credit to sources and furnish accuracy, reliability and authority to papers.
Thesis	Being able to narrow the topic into a clearly stated, direct, concise sentence which relays that topic to the reader.
Outlining	Being able to arrange content into a logical, orderly sequence proving the thesis and permitting the reader to understand what has been written.
Producing a readable paper	Being able to mold all of the information, ideas, words, and mechanics into a smooth, well-ordered paper.
Revision	Being able to assemble all elements of the research process into a polished, refined product.

After you have become acquainted with these skills through reading the chapters in this book, you will be asked to write a paper similar to "Help for the Child Abuser" and the other papers following the research assignments at the end of this book. The requirements of the assignment will be carefully detailed, and topics which have already been limited will be suggested. Only through active practice will you become skillful in producing a research paper. As a bonus, you will undoubtedly discover your own answer to the question, "What Is Research?"

The Planning and the Process

Library

Students who take time to acquaint themselves with library services and resources save valuable hours throughout their school years. At any rate, the student writing a research paper has little choice but to use the library, and learning to use it efficiently will conserve time, prevent frustration, and result in a rewarding paper.

Every library has a history of its own, and the researcher should acquaint himself with that history to prevent making some very basic mistakes. For instance, find out when your library was built. Some newer school libraries may have volumes dating back only ten to twelve years. Such information could be valuable when you are researching topics of historical significance.

Knowing how many volumes and periodicals your library contains may not help your research, but it may caution you against telling your instructor you "couldn't find a thing in that library." Even small libraries may contain an average of 42,000 volumes and subscribe to 600 periodicals. In addition to printed materials, there are usually microfilms, maps, microfilm readers, records, copy machines, and a variety of audio-visual equipment available. Find out if your library has any cooperative agreements with other local libraries or if it is a member of a district or state library system. If so, more resources will be available to you through interlibrary loans. Of course you may also need to utilize city, county, or state libraries in surrounding communities.

Most libraries publish guidebooks or pamphlets explaining the rules, hours, filing system, and location of materials. If your library does not publish this information, fill in the information below:

1. What are the library hours?
   a. Days.

b. Evenings.
c. Weekends.

2. Who are the reference librarians?

3. What are the requirements for borrowing books?
a. Identification required.
b. Length of loan period for:
(1) Circulation books.
(2) Reserve materials.
(3) Periodicals.

4. Location of outdoor book return.

5. Fines and penalties.

6. What library filing system is used to classify books? (Dewey Decimal System or Library of Congress.)

7. How does that system classify books? List the subject areas and their locating symbol.

8. Are the stacks open or closed?

9. Where can you locate the listing of periodicals contained in your library?

10. Are catalog cards filed in one alphabetized catalog, or in catalogs divided according to subject, author, and title?

ARRANGEMENT OF LIBRARY

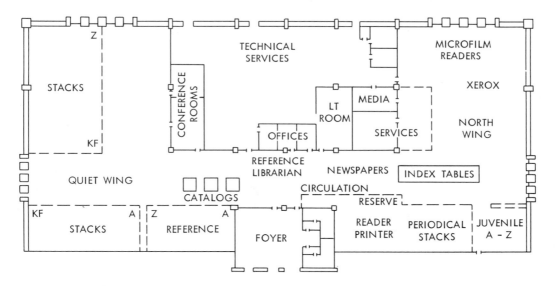

Fig. 2. A typical layout of a small school library.

Fill the map on page 16 with the layout of your library. It may serve as a ready guide for locating materials.

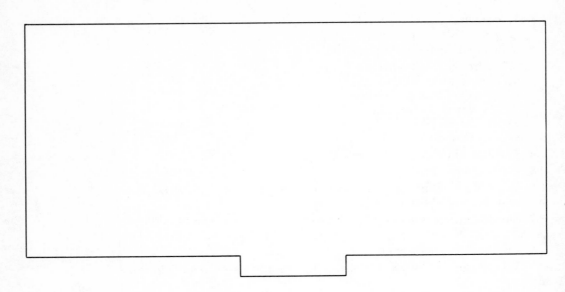

Basically, libraries provide three types of printed materials for reading, study, and research.

1. General books. These are usually available on open shelves or in closed stacks and borrowed for a specific period of time.

2. Reference works. A wealth of general information is contained in the reference section. The works include dictionaries, yearbooks. directories, almanacs and vertical file. These works do not circulate and must be used in the library.

3. Periodicals. Magazines and journals in regular bindings or on microfilm may be located in closed stacks.

HOW TO BEGIN

When the research assignment has been made, students often have difficulty knowing where to begin. A basic rule is to investigate how much material and what kinds of materials are available on the topic in your library. A good starting place is an encyclopedia. An encyclopedia may provide a concise overall view of the topic. Other reference books also provide information or serve as reference to other materials.

Caution: Avoid using more than one encyclopedia or taking extensive notes from the article. As a rule, encyclopedias will not afford the information necessary to *write* a paper and may stifle your writing style. Encyclopedias serve best by directing you to more complete treatments of the subject.

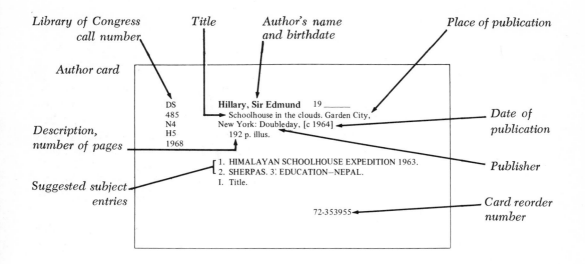

Library of Congress call number.

Title

Author's name and birthdate

Place of publication

Author card

Description, number of pages

Suggested subject entries

DS
485
N4
H5
1968

Hillary, Sir Edmund   19 _____
Schoolhouse in the clouds. Garden City,
New York: Doubleday, [c 1964]
192 p. illus.

1. HIMALAYAN SCHOOLHOUSE EXPEDITION 1963.
2. SHERPAS. 3. EDUCATION—NEPAL.
I. Title.

72-353955

Date of publication

Publisher

Card reorder number

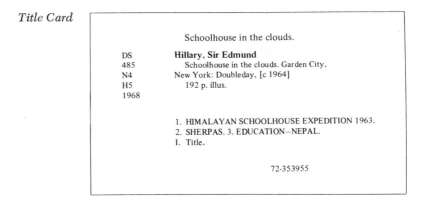

Title Card

Schoolhouse in the clouds.

DS
485
N4
H5
1968

Hillary, Sir Edmund
Schoolhouse in the clouds. Garden City,
New York: Doubleday, [c 1964]
192 p. illus.

1. HIMALAYAN SCHOOLHOUSE EXPEDITION 1963.
2. SHERPAS. 3. EDUCATION—NEPAL.
I. Title.

72-353955

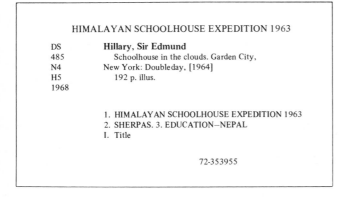

Subject card

HIMALAYAN SCHOOLHOUSE EXPEDITION 1963

DS
485
N4
H5
1968

Hillary, Sir Edmund
Schoolhouse in the clouds. Garden City,
New York: Doubleday, [1964]
192 p. illus.

1. HIMALAYAN SCHOOLHOUSE EXPEDITION 1963
2. SHERPAS. 3. EDUCATION—NEPAL
I. Title

72-353955

Fig. 3. Samples of library catalog cards.

THE CARD CATALOG

The most useful and most used tool in the library is the card catalog. The card catalog is an index to the library. It lists in alphabetical order, according to an elaborate filing system, the contents of the whole library. The two filing systems most frequently used are the Dewey Decimal System and the Library of Congress System. Most libraries utilize a catalog divided into three separate cabinets: the subject catalog, the author catalog, and the title catalog. Although students are accustomed to locating call number, subject, and author from a catalog card, additional information is also available as shown in Figure 3 on page 17.

Notice the call number in the upper left-hand corner. This number will direct you to the shelved books which are located in the stacks marked with that number.

PERIODICALS AND PERIODICAL INDEXES

Today students find that magazines, journals, and newspapers may contain the most useful up-to-date information in the library. While the names of the periodicals may appear in the card catalog, the titles of the individual articles do not. To locate articles on your subject, you will find a periodical index helpful. To beginning researchers, the most useful periodical index is *The Reader's Guide to Periodical Literature*.

The *Reader's Guide*, published since 1905, is an index to over a hundred different magazines. The arrangement of the *Reader's Guide* resembles that of a card catalog in that an article is listed under author's name, under subject heading, and by title. This enormous index requires an extensive system of abbreviations which may be unintelligible to you unless you become familiar with the legend listed at the beginning of each volume.

EXERCISE I   The following is a sample from the April 1953–February 1955 *Reader's Guide*, p. 811. Select four of the articles dealing with Mount Everest and decipher all the abbreviations. You will need to go to the library and consult the legend in the *Reader's Guide*. Then put the complete information into the following form:

1. Full name of author or authors.
2. Title of article properly marked.
3. Name of magazine properly underlined.
4. Publication data including volume and issue.
5. Page number or numbers.

EVEREST, Mount—*Continued*
Everest's conquerors come back. il map Life
35:120-9+ Jl 13 '53
Eyes on the stars; review of Mount Everest
reconnaissance expedition, by E. Shipton,
and Story of Everest, by W. H. Murray.
F. C. Lane. il Sat R 36:16-17 Jl 11 '53
Forerunners to Everest, by R. Dittert and
others. Review
Natur Hist 63:388+ N '54. E. T. Gilliard
Highest mountain in the world. Commonweal
58:193 My 29 '53
Mount Everest conquered. Time 61:35 Je 8 '53
Mt Everest mystery. H. Weinstock. il map
Holiday 13:107-8+ My '53
Movie camera's role in conquering Everest.
T. Stobart. il Photography 34:112+ Ap '54
Sunrise on Everest. A. Moorehead. il map
Atlan 194:109-11 N '54
Tensing of Everest; ed. by R. G. Hubler.
N. G. Dyhrenfurth. Harper 208:50-6 Mr '54
Triumph on Everest. J. Hunt; E. Hillary. il
map diags Nat Geog Mag 106:1-63 Jl '54
Why climb mountains? J. Hunt. il Rotarian
85:28-30 S '54
Will they climb Mt Everest now? E. Ship-
ton. il Colliers 131:11-15 Ap 4 '53
EVERETT, Edward G.
Summer of fear. Am Heritage 5 no2:26-7+
[D] '53
EVERETT, Ray Henry
Dreams can come true; poem. Nat Educ
Assn J 43:78 F '54 [1]

Another useful periodical index is the *New York Times Index*. This set of volumes indexes newspaper articles published in the *New York Times* since 1851. It is useful in dating an event even if the actual newspaper article is not available. The following excerpt from the 1962 *New York Times Index*, p. 631,[2] may provide practice in using the tool.

MOUNTAIN Climbing

Brit expedition led by Sir John Hunt to make attempt on Pamirs, USSR; map, Ja 10,5:4; Swiss guides H von Allmen and W Etter complete 1st winter ascent of Matterhorn north face; illus; map, F 5, 1:2; descend safely with 5-man Austrian-Ger team who also made ascent, F 7,39:4; 9 expeditions from 6 countries on way to Himalayas, Nepal, Ap 8,34:4; Indian Army expedition led by Maj Rana scales Kokthang, Sikkim, Ap 29,26:1; Japan repts record 160 killed, 277 hurt, '61, 62% above '60, My 6,23:2; Brit Royal Marines to attempt Mt McKinley without oxygen, My 7,2:8; French team scales Mt Jannu, Nepal, My 9,4:6

Japanese team in Nepal; scales Hongde peak (22,212 ft), Mukut Himal range, My 16,34:1; scales 23,240-ft Jugal Himal, My 18,2:4; reptd scaling Nupchu peak, My 29,7:6

US team starts Gyachungking climb, Nepal, My 28,22:2

Indian Army team forced back by storm 400 ft from Everest summit; W Ger team scales Pumori peak, Nepal, Je 3,3:6; Brit women's team scales Kanjiroba Himal, Nepal, Je 5,10:5; Sir John Hunt to head Brit team attempt to scale Communism Peak, highest in USSR (25,000 ft), Je 6,7:1; 2 on Everest team frostbitten; flown to New Delhi, Je 7,3:3

Sir John Hunt says he will probably not undertake major climbs again, Ag 3,4:4; Appalachian Mt Club admits 10 members failed to register for Grand Teton Mt climb, hearing; Boston Club agrees to pay rescue expenses; case dismissed, Ag 5,9:1; 3-man Japanese-Pakistani team scales Saltoro Kangri peak, Pakistan, Ag 9,2:2; L Kor and C Roskosz scale eastern face of Long's Peak, Colo, Ag 13, 21:1; 2 Itals claim 1st ascent of Matterhorn west wall, Ag 15,12:7

4 Siberians scale previously unclimbed peak in Tien Shan Mts, near Chinese Turkestan, Ag 16,7:1; Brit-USSR team scales Mt Communism (24,590 ft), highest in USSR; Brit are 1st foreigners to scale it; map, Ag 17,2:5; comment on hazards to climbers, Alps Mont Blanc range; new cable cars take tourists to climbing areas, Ag 26,16:3

6 scale north wall of Mt Eiger, Swiss Alps; 2 others killed in attempt, S 1,5:2; 12 unidentified climbers attempt Eiger, S 4,4:5; J Olsen book on unsuccessful '57 attempt on Eiger north wall revd, S 9,VII,p12; Sir Edmund Hillary and D Doig book on their '60 Himalayan expedition revd, O 21,VII,p38; Alps '62 death toll at 239, lowest in 6 yrs, N 4,2:4

US 19-man team led by N G Dyhrenfurth and Dr W Siri plan attempts on Mts Everest, Lhotse and Nuptse, May '63; partly financed by grants from govt groups, Natl Geographic Soc and UCLA, who spon-

EXERCISE II   Select an article on mountain climbing. Then refer to a volume of the index for the legend to abbreviations and answer the following questions:

1. What date was the article published?
2. In what periodical was the article published?
3. What points were discussed in the article?

Biographical Reference Works

Frequently subjects deal with people or personalities. The *Biography Index*, published since 1946, can be helpful in locating articles, books, and magazines on individuals. For example, Heinrich Schliemann's involvement with Troy makes him an important person.

EXERCISE III   The following information can be found in the September 1955–August 1958 *Biography Index*, p. 743. Locate Heinrich Schliemann's name and answer the following. Once again you should consult a volume of the index for directions on how to use it efficiently.

SCHLESINGER, Arthur Meier, 1917- historian
  Biography
    Sat R por 40:11 Mr 2 '57
  Kunitz, Stanley Jasspon, ed. Twentieth century authors; 1st sup. Wilson '55 p877-8 bibliog por
SCHLIEKER, Willy Hermann, 1914?- German steel executive
  Four who made it—big. il por Newsweek 49: 77-80 Je 3 '57
SCHLIEMANN, Heinrich, 1822-1890, German archeologist
  Grigson, Geoffrey, and Gibbs-Smith, C. H. eds. People. Hawthorn '56 p376-7
  Padover, Saul Kussiel, ed. Confessions and self-portraits. Day '57 p211-14

        Juvenile literature
  Hume, Ivor Noël. Great moments in archaeology. Roy '58 p49-62 il
SCHLODIEN, Nikolaus, burggraf zu Dohna- See Dohna-Schlodien, N.
SCHLOSS, Oscar Menderson, 1882-1952, physician
  Gordon, H. H. Oscar Menderson Schloss. (In Veeder, Borden Smith, ed. Pediatric profiles. Mosby '57 p202-10) por
SCHLUMBERGER, Jean, French jeweler
  D'Otrange-Mastai, M. L. Jean Schlumberger: creator of jewels. il Apollo 61:164-71 Je '55
SCHLUNDT, Herman, 1869-1937, chemist
  Biography 3

[3] Material from *Biography Index* reproduced by permission of The H. W. Wilson Company.

1. What information is given about his background?
2. What articles can be located about him?
   Where can they be found?
3. What books can be located about him?
   Where can they be found?

Numerous biographical dictionaries are available that provide useful information on celebrities living and dead. Some of the best known are *Current Biography, The Dictionary of American Biography, The Dictionary of National Biography,* and *Who's Who.* These and more are available in the reference section of the library.

Academic References

Reference works of all kinds are available for use in academic fields. *The Education Index,* published since 1929, is one example of an index to articles on and about education.

MULTIPURPOSE rooms
  Ideas by design: uncommon commons; Cleveland, Tex; high school. il Nations Sch & Coll 2:46 Mr '75
  Turn for the better: revolving shells at Juanita high school, Kirkland, Wash. il Nations Sch & Coll 2:40 Ja '75
MULTISENSORY learning. See Learning, Psychology of—Perceptual learning
MULTITRAIT-multimethod matrix. See Tests and scales—Validity—Construct validity
MULTI-UNIT schools. See Administration of schools—Elementary schools
MULTIVARIATE analysis. See Statistical methods
MULTIVARIATE analysis of variance. See Analysis of variance
MULTIVARIATE designs. See Experimental design
MUMMIES
  Mummy of mystery. Intellect 103:150-1 D '74
MUMPS
  Children in educational programs for the hearing impaired whose impairment was caused by mumps. C. Jensema. J Speech & Hearing Dis 40:164-9 My '75
MUNDEL, David S.
  Financing higher education: the current state of the debate; comment. Liberal Educ 60 supp:55-60 Mr '74
MUNDT, John
  State NVATA role: keeping members informed. por Agric Educ Mag 46:111 N '73
MUNDY, C. Jean
  Performance based contract teaching. JOHPER 45:39-40 O '74
MUNICIPAL employees
  Some characteristics of inaccessible respondents in a telephone survey. C. N. Weaver and others. J App Psychol 60:260-2 Ap '75
    See also
  American federation of state, county and municipal employees [4]

[4] *Education Index.* Copyright © 1975 The H. W. Wilson Company. Material reproduced by permission of the publisher.

EXERCISE IV   From the following excerpt, locate an article about mummies. Then, using a key to the abbreviations used in the index, answer the following questions:

1. In what work does the article appear?
2. What is the title of the article?
3. Who is the author?

REFERENCE WORKS

The wealth of information available in reference works constitutes a researcher's bonanza. General reference works and specialized reference works are located in a separate reference room or on a section of shelves designated as the reference area. The hundreds of references published require that the beginning researcher acquaint himself with what is available. Librarians may provide bibliographies of the references contained in the library or references may be located under appropriate subject areas in the card catalog. Take a browsing tour among the reference shelves and note the numerous titles and academic areas contained there for future reference. The following list presents a limited look at reference works available. Remember the references listed are only a few of those available in each area.

General Reference Works

1. **Atlases**—collections of maps.
   Hammond Medallion World Atlas. Maplewood, N.J.: C. S. Hammond, 1971.
   National Atlas of the United States. Washington, D.C.: Government Printing Office, 1970.
2. **Bibliographies of Reference Works**
   Barton, Mary N. *Reference Books: A Brief Guide for Students and Other Users of the Library.* 6th rev. ed. Baltimore: Enoch Pratt Library, 1966.
   Murphy, Robert W. *How and Where to Look It Up.* New York: McGraw-Hill Book Co., 1958.
   Shores, Louis. *Basic Reference Sources.* Chicago: American Library Association, 1954.
3. **Biography**
   Biography Index 1947–. An index to books and articles about public figures.

   Current Biography 1940–. Articles about living persons.
   Dictionary of American Biography. 20 vols. New York: Scribners, 1928–73. Articles about deceased American leaders.

Dictionary of National Biography. 63 vols. London: Smith, Elder, 1885–1950. Biographical information on deceased English citizens.

Who's Who. London: Black, 1849–.

4. **Dictionaries**—information on history and origin of words in addition to information on spelling, pronunciation, and definition.

A New English Dictionary on Historical Principles. 10 vols. Oxford: Clarendon Press, 1884–1933 (issued in 1933 as *The Oxford English Dictionary*).

Funk and Wagnalls New Practical Standard Dictionary of the English Language. New York: Funk & Wagnalls, 1964.

Webster's New Dictionary of Synonyms. Springfield, Mass.: G. and C. Merriam, 1968.

5. **Encyclopedias**—useful for exploring all subjects.

Collier's Encyclopedia. 24 vols. New York: Crowell-Collier. (Continuously updated.)

Encyclopaedia Britannica. 24 vols. Chicago: Encyclopedia Britannica, Inc.

Van Nostrand's Scientific Encyclopedia. 4th ed. New York: Van Nostrand Reinhold, 1968.

6. **Gazetteers**—dictionaries of places.

Columbia-Lippincott Gazetteer of the World. 2nd ed. New York: Columbia University Press, 1962.

7. **Government Publications**

Andriot, John L. *Guide to U.S. Government Serials and Periodicals.* 3 vols. 1962.

Vertical File Index. 1932–. Lists pamphlets and booklets by subject.

8. **Indexes**—directories to sources containing discussion about a subject. *The Reader's Guide, Biography Index, New York Times Index,* and *Education Index* are discussed elsewhere in this section. A thorough knowledge of indexes is especially useful.

Applied Science and Technology Index, 1958–.

Book Review Digest. New York, 1905–.

Essay and General Literature Index. New York: H. W. Wilson, 1934–.

Poole's Index to Periodical Literature. 6 vols. Boston: Houghton Mifflin, 1888–1908.

Public Affairs Information Service, 1915–.

9. **Quotation Dictionaries**

Bartlett, John. *Familiar Quotations.* 14th ed. Boston: Little, Brown, 1968.

Stevenson, Burton E. *The Home Book of Quotations, Classical and Modern.* 10th ed. New York: Dodd, Mead, 1967.

10. **Yearbooks**—useful resources for facts, figures, and statistics.

Annual Register of World Events: A Review of the Year. London: Longmans Green, 1758–.

Facts on File. 1940–. (Weekly news digest and semimonthly cumulative index.)

The Guinness Book of World Records. 11th ed. New York: Sterling, 1972.

The World Almanac and Book of Facts. New York: Doubleday, 1968–.

Reference Works in Specialized Areas

1. **Art**
   Chamberlin, Mary W. *Guide to Art Reference Books.* Chicago: American Library Association, 1959.
   Encyclopedia of World Art. 15 vols. New York: McGraw-Hill, 1939.
2. **Business**
   Business Periodicals Index. 1958–.
3. **History, American**
   Guide to the Study of the United States of America. Washington, D.C.: Library of Congress, 1960.
4. **History, World**
   Cambridge Modern History. 13 vols. New York: Cambridge University Press, 1902–26.
5. **Literary Aids**
   Granger's Index to Poetry. 5th ed. New York: Columbia University Press, 1962.
   Walker, Warren S. *Twentieth Century Short Story Explication.* 2nd ed. Hamden, Conn.: Shoe String Press, 1967.
6. **Literature, American**
   Van Doren, Carl, and others, eds. *Cambridge History of American Literature.* 4 vols. New York: G. P. Putnam, 1917–21.
   Hart, James. *Oxford Companion to American Literature.* New York: Oxford University Press, 1965.
7. **Literature, English**
   Cambridge History of English Literature. 15 vols. New York: G. P. Putnam, 1939.
   Harvey, Sir Paul. *Oxford Companion to English Literature.* New York: Oxford University Press, 1967.
8. **Music**
   Grove, Sir George. *Dictionary of Music and Musicians.* 5th ed. 10 vols. New York: St. Martin's Press, 1970.
9. **Mythology and Folklore**
   Bullfinch's Mythology. New York: T. Y. Crowell, 1970.
   Mythology of All Races. 13 vols. Boston: Archaeological Institute, 1916–32.
10. **Philosophy**
    The Encyclopedia of Philosophy. 8 vols. New York: Macmillan, 1967.

11. Psychology

Drever, James. *A Dictionary of Psychology.* Rev. ed. Baltimore: Penguin Books, 1971.

12. Religion

Adams, Charles J. *A Reader's Guide to the Great Religions.* New York: Free Press, 1965.

Index to Religious Periodical Literature. 1949–.

13. Science, General

McGraw-Hill Encyclopedia of Science and Technology. 15 vols. New York: 1966.

Singer, Charles, and E. J. Holmyard. *A History of Technology.* 5 vols. New York: Oxford University Press, 1954.

14. Sociology

American Journal of Sociology. 1895–.

15. Sports

Menke, Frank G. *The Encyclopedia of Sports.* New York: A. S. Barnes, 1953.

16. Theatre

Hartnoll, Phyllis. *Oxford Companion to the Theatre.* New York: Oxford University Press, 1967.

Bibliography

One of the distinguishing features of a research paper is the acknowledgement of sources in a list called a bibliography. A bibliography itemizes, in an alphabetically arranged list, all sources actually used in compiling the paper. The purpose of the bibliography is to provide the reader with information should he wish to read further on the subject.

From the moment you locate a book or article you want to use in your research, write all of the basic information about it on a 3 × 5 card. You may rely upon some sources quite heavily. Other sources may supply only minimal information or background, and you may discard others. Only those sources actually used should appear in the final bibliography at the end of your paper.

To ensure consistency of style among academic or published writings, the Modern Language Association has established guidelines for bibliographies and footnotes. These guidelines, published as the *MLA Style Sheet,* have been widely accepted and encourage uniformity in academic writing. A bibliography, therefore, has a standard form and you will save time by writing the entries properly on your bibliography card the first time you locate the book or article. Books and magazines are cited in different ways and these forms should be adhered to on your bibliography card. In a simple college research paper the following rules are necessary when listing a book in a bibliography.

1. The author's name in reversed order so it can be arranged alphabetically according to the last name. The name is followed by a period.

2. Full title of the book *underlined,* followed by a period.

3. The city, publisher, and date of publication followed by a period.

4. The call number, which is optional, is placed in the upper left-hand corner.

```
DS          Hillary, Sir Edmund. Schoolhouse in
485             the Clouds. Garden City, New
N4              York: Doubleday & Co., Inc.,
                1964.
```

A bibliography card for a magazine article with and without an author consists of:

With an author

```
Hunt, Sir John. "Triumph on Everest."
    The National Geographic, 106
    (July 1954), 64.
```

Without an author

```
"The Conquest of Everest."
    Life, 29 June 1953, pp. 42-43.
```

1. The author's full name in reversed order, followed by a period. If author's name is not given begin citation with the title of the article.

2. The full title of the article enclosed in quotation marks and followed by a period.

3. The full title of the magazine or encyclopedia *underlined* and followed by a comma.

4. The issue of the magazine and the page numbers. (This is discussed in the following paragraphs.)

Since magazine volume numbers may be omitted or included according to the writer's preference, special consideration is required for this information. A growing trend is to omit volume number and use the military style of dating, for it simplifies punctuation. Entries should consist of:

Magazine citation
with a volume number

McGourin, Thomas. "How to Write a
Term Paper." *Black Collegian,*
6 (Jan./Feb. 1976), 14–15.

or

"Nobody Asked: Is It Moral?" *Time,*
107 (10 May 1976), 32.

or

"Nobody Asked: Is It Moral?" *Time,*
107 (May 10, 1976), 32.

1. The magazine name followed by a comma.

2. The volume number indicated by an Arabic or a Roman numeral.

3. Parentheses containing the date and followed by a comma.

4. The page numbers listed *without* any abbreviation for the word page or pages, and the citation ended with a period.

Magazine citation
without a volume number

McGourin, Thomas. "How to Write a
Term Paper." *Black Collegian,*
Jan./Feb. 1976, pp. 14–15.

or

"Nobody Asked: Is It Moral?" *Time,*
10 May 1976, p. 32.

or

"Nobody Asked: Is It Moral?" *Time,*
May 10, 1976, p. 32.

1. The magazine name followed by a comma.

2. The date written in military style or conventional style, followed by a comma.

3. The abbreviation p. or pp. preceding page number or numbers and the citation ending with a period.

Caution: Choose the method of recording volume number that you prefer, then use it consistently. Do not mix methods.

The following sample of a *final bibliography* adheres to the basic rules for arrangement of data:

Bibliography

Bratton, Fred Gladstone. A History of Egyptian
    Archaeology. New York: Thomas Y. Crowell, 1968.

Cooney, John D. "Egypt's Pyramids." Science, Sept. 1961, pp. 60-68.

"Pyramids." World Book Encyclopedia (1970). VI, 810-11.

Scheller, Ronald. "Unsolved Mysteries of the
    Great Pyramids." Reader's Digest, Dec. 1974, pp. 140-44.

Von Daniken, Erich. Chariots of the Gods.
    New York: Bantam Books, 1968.

_____. Gold of the Gods. Boston: Putnam, 1973.

Wright, James D. Egypt. Boston: Barclay House, 1975.

---

1. List all works in alphabetical order according to the author's last name. For works with no author (alphabetize according to the first word of the title except A, An, and The. (Bibliography items are not numbered.)

2. Place all of the bibliographic citation on one line if possible. If the citation requires more than one line, indent the second line five spaces.

3. Place periods between each of the three basic information units, i.e.:
    a. author's name (period)
    b. title (period)
    c. publication data (period)

4. Bibliographies are usually single spaced within the citation and double spaced between citations.

5. If you have two or more books or articles written by the same author, alphabetize the bibliography citation by titles. Instead of repeating the name of the author each time after the first citation, insert a line approximately one inch long where the name would normally appear.

6. No page numbers are required for books; however, periodicals must show page numbers for the entire article.

To illustrate how all forms of bibliographic entries should be written is impractical here, but the following models illustrate the most commonly used materials. Note: Wherever printers use italics to indicate titles or foreign words or phrases, students should identify this information in their papers by underlining.

Models of Bibliography Citations

1. Anonymous Author

Magazine articles are frequently unsigned by an author. Do not use the word "anonymous" unless it appears on the title page of the article. The military method of writing the date simplifies punctuation.

"New Outlook for the Aged." *Time,* 2 June 1975, pp. 44–51.

2. Anthology

An anthology is a collection of articles written by one author or many different authors bound into a single volume. It is treated much like a periodical citation in that it lists the title of the article as well as the name of the volume.

Orwell, George. "Politics and the English Language" in a *Collection of Essays.* Garden City: Doubleday, 1954.

3. Bible

A valuable source of quotations, history, and philosophy, the Bible is frequently cited. Neither the Bible nor books of the Bible are underlined or enclosed in quotation marks. The Bible is usually identified by book, chapter, and verse in Arabic numbers.

Matthew 6:1–8.

4. Book

Angelou, Maya. *Gather Together in My Name.* New York: Random House, 1974.

5. Classic Literature

For classics and widely known literary works by authors long deceased, such as Shakespeare or Homer, the author's name may be omitted or more complete information referring to a particular edition or translation may be given.

As You Like It, II, vii, 70–77.

Iliad, IV, 12.

Shakespeare, William. *Hamlet.* New York: Washington Square Press, 1957.

The Illiad of Homer. Trans. Richard Lattimore. Chicago, Illinois: The University of Chicago Press, 1961.

6. Co-authors

Names of collaborating authors should be recorded in the same order as they appear on the title page. The first author's name is reversed for purposes of alphabetizing, and the second author's name appears in regular order.

Sommer, Barbara, and Robert Sommer. "The Best Are Waste." *Nation,* 219 (19 October 1974), 369–372.

Brerland, Cottie, and Irene Nicholson. *Mythology of the Americans.* New York: Hamlyn, 1970.

7. Editor

Works compiled by an editor may consist of writings by others. The editor is given credit in the following way:

Lodge, Henry Cabot, ed. *History of Nations.* New York: Collier Press, 1913.

8. Encyclopedias

Encyclopedia articles are seldom signed by an author. The alphabetical arrangement of the book presents little difficulty for a reader looking for a particular subject. A usual citation is:

"Vampires." *Encyclopedia Americana* (1973), XXVII, 876.

9. Government Documents

The ever-increasing up-to-date information provided by the government printing service provides an abundance of current knowledge. Typical government documents carry special catalog or report numbers which should be included.

Davis, Frederick B., ed. *The Army Air Force Qualifying Examination.* Army Air Force Psychology Program, Report No. 6 (Washington, D.C. U.S. Government Printing Office, 1947), pp. 53–55.

Congressional Record

Some government documents are issued periodically, such as the following:

"Petitions and Memorials." *Congressional Record,* 25 February 1956, p. 3456.

10. Interview

Much modern research is accomplished by talking, formally or informally, with recognized authors, specialists, or other individuals.

Howe, Dr. Helena. Personal interview concerning Mesa Community College. Mesa, Arizona, June 1975.

11. Letters

Letters may serve as authoritative and informative material for research. Letters of famous personalities are often preserved as historical documents, but even everyday correspondence may contain useful facts.

Sheeler, Dr. J. Reuben. Personal letter. 6 June 1975.

12. Magazines

The military syle of dating simplifies punctuation.

With an author and without volume number:

Moss, Robert F. "The Arts in Black America." *Saturday Review,* 15 November 1975, pp. 12–19.

Without an author and without volume number:

"Nobody Asked: Is It Moral?" *Time,* 10 May 1976, p. 32.

Without an author and with a volume number:

"Nobody Asked: Is It Moral?" *Time,* 107 (10 May 1976), 32.

13. Multiple Authors

Works to which numerous authors have contributed may be listed under the major author's name with the phrase "and others." The use of the Latin phrase *et al.*, while becoming less common, may also be used.

Campbell, James S., and others. *Law and Order Reconsidered*. New York: Bantam Books, 1970.

14. Multiple Volumes

In a set of books, the reader must be directed to the specific volume or made aware that more than one volume exists.

Carter, Howard, and A. C. Mack. *The Tomb of Tutankhamen*. 3 vols. Philadelphia: Cooper Square Publisher, 1963.

Sandburg, Carl. *Abraham Lincoln*. Vol. V. New York: Harcourt Brace, 1939.

15. Newspapers

Daily publication of newspapers makes them essential sources for research. Newspapers may or may not carry a by-line of the author. If the author's name is given, list it. Title may be listed if it is available and of significance to the research.

The Arizona Republic (Phoenix), 8 June 1975, p. 1–A (or Sec. A, p. 1).

Jensen, Conrad, "Phoenician Backpacks into Lofty Himalayas." *The Arizona Republic*, 8 June 1975, p. N–8 (or Sec. N, p. 8).

16. Pamphlets

Students are discovering that pamphlets serve as important sources for research. Agencies, organizations, businesses, and associations publish pamphlets dealing with their specialized interests. However, this assortment of authors makes for confusing bits of information when writing the citation. The writer may at times have to rely upon his judgment to write a clear and orderly citation. The abbreviation n.d. (no date) and n.p. (no publisher) may be used when date and publisher are unavailable.

American Council on Education. *College Teaching as a Career*. Washington, D.C.: American Council on Education, 1958.

17. Specific Edition

Books may be revised numerous times after the first publication to keep information current, add new material, or change format. The writer must advise the reader of the edition used.

Lucas, Alfred. *Ancient Egyptian Materials and Industries*. 4th rev. ed. New York: St. Martin's Press, 1962.

18. Unpublished Manuscript

College libraries maintain collections of unpublished master's theses and doctoral dissertations useful for research.

Inglish, Ida Joyce. "The English Decadence and the Satirist." (Unpublished doctoral dissertation in the Arizona State University Library), 1967.

19. Untitled Article

Arizona Days and Ways. 8 June 1975, p. 30.

Reading, Sorting, and Note-Taking

After selecting the subject for your research paper, but before taking notes, you should acquire some knowledge of the topic through broad, general reading. You might start with an encyclopedia article if the subject is indexed there. If the encyclopedia has no listing close to the subject, you might select two or three articles, or a portion of a book. You are not at this time searching for specifics, but for a feel of the subject, an understanding of its divisions and limits. Through the perusal of such materials, you should be able to place the subject in its historical and cultural setting. If the subject is an event such as the sinking of the *Titanic*, the assassination of President Lincoln, or the ascent of Mount Everest, become familiar with when, where, and why it happened. If the subject is a person, find out when and where that person lived, the major incidents in his life, his successes and failures. If the subject is a social problem, such as how to rehabilitate alcoholics or how to ensure quality education for bilingual children, then survey the history of the problem, its current status, what solutions have been tried, and what is being offered.

After you have learned enough about the subject to discuss it in general terms, begin limiting. By this time, you should have developed an interest in, should be curious about, or intrigued by certain portions of the subject. With your interests narrowed, you can begin to be more selective in reading portions of books and more limited articles. You are now ready to begin thinking about taking notes.

At this point, you begin the foundation for a successful research paper. Set yourself a procedure and follow it:

1. Before taking any notes from an article or book chapter, *read the article or chapter completely*. You will then have a firmer idea of what material will be useful. Extensive copying of sources only partially digested results in stacks of note cards, but often in little usable material. Recognizing what facts and opinions will be needed is sometimes difficult and too much is preferable to too little, but your time is precious and should not be wasted.

2. Make a bibliography card before taking any notes. This card must contain full information about the book, article, or pamphlet. See bibliography section for a complete discussion of bibliographical forms.

3. Take notes on 4 × 6 cards, one subject heading per card. Notes taken in a notebook or on sheets of paper are unmanageable because they cannot be easily rearranged according to subject headings (labels) when developing the outline, or according to outline when writing the paper.

The note card must contain the following information:

    a. Source of material.
    b. Page number or numbers on which the material is found.
    c. A label or heading for the material.
    d. The material, correctly identified as quotation, summary, list, etc.

In the upper right-hand corner of the card, indicate the source by the author's last name, the title of the book or article, and the page number. In the upper left-hand corner, place the label. Below are sample cards used for the paper "The Humbling of Everest."

C	**A**	**B**
Sherpas' Duties	White, *All About Mountains*	p. 116
D	1. Acted as porters — carried climbers' racks 2. Set up highest camps 3. Cooked 4. Looked after equipment They felt as part of a team.	

A *Source*

B *Page number*

C *Label*

D *Material (information)*

4. Summarize the material in your own words most of the time. *Beware of extensive quotation!* Summarizing will save time both while you are taking notes and later while you are writing the paper. It will prevent you from boring your reader with numerous quoted passages which he will skip if possible. It will also eliminate the possibility of *plagiarism.*

Plagiarism is copying another writer's words and passing them off as your own. It is substituting a word here and there, but following another

C	A	B
Everest Team	*Milne, Mountains p.20*	

D *Smoothly functioning, forged by Colonel Hunt, whose "firm conviction that by striving one for all and all for one they might prevail, and then only if Everest gave them the luck of the weather."*

A *Source*
B *Page number*
C *Label*
D *Material (information)*

writer's train of thought. It is lifting choice phrases and inserting them into your sentences. *Plagiarism is stealing.*

5. Quote only when there is a definite reason for quoting: when you need the exact words of an authority; when citing passages from letters, diaries, legal documents; when a particular piece of description will develop a point vividly and exactly. Most readers pass over or skim quoted passages unless they are inextricably integrated into the thought of the paper. Nothing makes for more tiresome, unrewarding reading than a patchwork of quotations.

6. Put notes from each source on individual cards. Recording one idea per card ensures ease of arrangement. Make certain that all material on the card is related to the card's label, because these labels will help you develop your outline and may be organized to follow your outline when you are writing the paper. It is essential to include the page number on each note card at the time you record the information to ensure that the location of the material will be accurately recorded in documentation.

Documentation: In-Text

Whenever the writer borrows ideas, facts, statistics, or opinions from the author of an article, newspaper, magazine column, or book, or from a radio or television commentator or any other authority, he should give the source credit. Giving credit to a source for evidence, proof, or information is called *documentation*. The writer wants these materials in his paper because they support the points he is making. These borrowed facts or opinions help to convince the reader that the ideas expressed in the paper have validity and substance. This validity or substance is reinforced when the writer cites his source's name, qualifications, and the place where the material can be found. Citing of sources helps the reader to progress smoothly through the text, to grasp the ideas, to recognize the authenticity of the information, to rely on the credibility of the writer. The material cited may be a summary of ideas, a list of points, or a quotation. To keep accurate records of this material, the writer should record the information on note cards.

Sources are commonly acknowledged in one of two ways:

1. Acknowledgement may be incorporated in the text of a paper.
2. Acknowledgements may be included as footnotes to the text.

In-text documentation operates smoothly when a paper is relatively short and only a few sources are used. In a long paper based on many sources, in-text documentation may become unwieldy. In such a paper, footnotes may be more effective. Footnotes will be discussed in the next chapter.

When citing sources in your text, you should make smooth transitions and vary sentence structure to avoid tiresome or mechanical repetition. For example, the following note cards were made from the article, "When a Child Has Trouble in School" published in the October 1974 issue of *Woman's Day* magazine. This information was recorded on a bibliography card (Card A).

Chess, Stella, M.D. "When a Child Has Trouble in School." Woman's Day, 38 (Oct. 1974), 76, 150–152.

Card A

Bibliography card

After reading the article, the student recorded the material on note cards. These notes summarized the information needed in four ways: as itemized points (Card B), short notes (Card C), lists of reasons (Card D), or quotation (Card E).

When writing the paper, the student constructed the following paragraph using in-text documentation from the itemized points on Card B.

> The parents of a child entering kindergarten or first grade should realize that he will certainly face adjustment problems. Most children learn to cope with these stresses and strains, but some children need help. Dr. Stella Chess, in "When a Child Has Trouble in School," October 1974, in *Woman's Day*, p. 76, suggests that parents be alerted if their child has difficulty learning to read or understanding what he has read. If the child interrupts classmates, does not pay attention, regresses to babyish behavior, or becomes overly sensitive, parents should not become alarmed but should become aware of potential learning barriers.

The paragraph below was constructed using the quotation on Card E.

> The unhappy child who dreads going to school, the belligerent child who abuses his classmates, the overly-dependent child who clings to his mother or father should neither be ignored nor bullied. He needs help from parents, teachers, and possibly a psychologist or pediatrician. Per-

Problems a Child May Have: Chess, p. 76

1. Learning to read
2. Not understanding what he has read
3. Interrupting classmates
4. Not paying attention
5. Acting younger than he is
6. Becoming overly sensitive

Regressive Behavior: Chess, p. 76

1. Bed wetting
2. Baby talk
3. Clinging to parents in public
4. Showing conflict and anxiety

Causes of anxiety: Chess, p. 150

1. Child may be pushed too hard
2. Child may not understand what he is
   supposed to do.
3. Child may be victim of a bully.
4. Child may feel a teacher is unfriendly.

Card D

Lists of reasons

Slow Learners — Hope for   Chess, p. 152

"Many normal children catch on slowly —
perhaps because we have not yet found the
best ways to help them learn. Children
who take longer to grasp new things learn
as well as other children ... they may become more serious scholars than some fast
learners."

Card E

Quotation

sistent behavioral disturbances demand parents' attention. But parents can take heart, because many of these disturbances right themselves and children who are apparently slow learners in the primary grades will catch up. These children "learn as well as other children" and may in the long run "become more serious scholars than some fast learners," according to Dr. Stella Chess in "When a Child Has Trouble in School," October 1974, *Woman's Day*, p. 152. She cautions parents to be concerned about their children, to be sympathetic, but not to waste time and energy in enervating worry.

In writing a paper utilizing information from other writers, you should remember to be courteous and honest. You must give credit where it is due.

PROPOSED MEDIUM SECURITY PRISON
FOR YOUNG ADULTS

The proposed center for young adults is desperately needed and long overdue; however, many people feel the center should be located where residents have expressed their endorsement and look forward to having the facility constructed within their community. Often people oppose locating such a facility in their immediate community for several reasons, some personal and some economic. Senator Leo Corbet urged a Maricopa County site in an article published in the *Arizona Republic* on 29 January 1975, p. 9, saying that "the citizens opposing the facilities are the same ones crying for action to fight crime."

JoAnne Williams

THE FACE-SAVING RATING SYSTEM

The X Rating is the last and strongest classification in the rating system. As Jack Longgath explains in "Doctor X," published in the 2 December 1972 issue of *Saturday Review*, p. 29, this is one rating which no industry wants. This classification is for movies containing items which should be viewed by adults only. Although the President's Commission on Obscenity and Pornography reports no evidence that sex promotes crime, members of the rating panel have decided these movies contain too much sex or violence to be viewed by anyone younger than twenty-one. Unlike PG and R, this classification has definite boundaries and it needs no revising.

Sherry Holmes

CREDIT CARDS: THE PLAGUE OF THE CONSUMER

Because of easy credit, many households overextend themselves financially and end up filing bankruptcy in courts now overflowing with such cases. Mr. Stan Benson from the National Foundation of Consumer

Credit was quoted as advocating consumer education in "Easy Credit Drives More Families to the Brink?" in the 15 July 1974 issue of *U.S. News & World Report,* p. 38. Mr. Benson feels "it's not so much that people are careless with credit but that they have never learned how to use it."

GLENDA HIGGINS

HOW MAY ALCOHOLICS BE HELPED?

According to Grace Naismith in "Antabuse Can Help Alcoholics" in the April 1974 issue of *Reader's Digest,* p. 60, an alcoholic who is properly motivated and supervised can kick the drinking habit with the aid of Antabuse. Antabuse is a drug discovered in 1947 by Eric Jacobson and Jens Hold, Danish biochemists. Antabuse blocks an enzyme in the liver necessary for complete metabolism of acetaldehyde. As acetaldehyde accumulates with alcohol, it causes toxic effects. The drug was approved by the Food and Drug Administration in 1951 and costs as little as seven cents per tablet.

JORI WRIGHT

Each of the preceding paragraphs cites one source through in-text documentation. More than one source may be cited in developing a paragraph:

Failure to communicate with others and form warm interpersonal relationships is perhaps the most serious cause of suicides. When a young person cannot communicate with others, he feels lonely and alienated and may resort to taking his own life. According to "Youthful Suicides," *Newsweek,* February 1971, p. 71, drugs and school pressures are not the prime reasons for teenage suicides. Studies of those attempting suicide show that pressures from parents and feelings of hopelessness were major contributors. Adolescents with no close friends, experiencing moods of isolation and loneliness, often try death as a means of escape. The lonelier the individuals, the more withdrawn they become, thus increasing their desolation. This vicious circle entraps the isolated individual. Figures published in "I Want Out," *Today's Health,* January 1971, p. 32, indicate that according to the U.S. Department of Health, Education, and Welfare, "one thousand boys and girls aged nineteen and younger commit suicide each year." In fact, only accidents and cancer kill more youths than does suicide. Suicide is a cry for help. Unfortunately, people tend to believe the old myth that a person who talks of suicide never actually goes through with it; but talking of suicide, one of the first warning signals, indicates a young person is calling for someone to pay attention. Other warning signals, as given in "Adolescent Suicide," *Time,* 3 January 1972, p. 57, are the following:

1. Insomnia
2. Not caring about appearance
3. Depression

4. Loss of appetite
5. Sudden upswing from depression

Certainly, those concerned about young people should be sensitive to their moods and ready to lend support when help is needed.

KATHIE MACDONALD

In the following paragraph, the student has cited three sources for the material. A source may be noted in one paragraph and referred to in a later one as is done in the following two paragraphs:

The Arabian Oryx, the antelope of the Middle East, has been captured and transported to the Phoenix Zoo to protect it from poachers and extinction. Its coat is a creamy white, with light brown markings on its head and legs. It has long, slender horns that may grow to twenty-nine inches. D. S. Henderson, author of "The Arabian Oryx: a Desert Tragedy," *National Parks and Recreation,* May 1974, p. 15, states that the horns of the Oryx "seem to grow from a common base" and "may be the origin of ancient tales of the mythological unicorn." This animal once roamed the sparsely vegetated, vast desert of the Saudi Arabian Peninsula and north into Sinai, Palestine, Jordan, Syria, and Iraq. Its territorial range has lessened as poachers depleted the "oryx-unicorn" population.

Such poaching has reduced the Arabian Oryx population to near extinction. According to "Unite for the Unicorn," *Newsweek,* 2 July 1962, p. 51, poachers use jeeps and Cadillacs to run down the antelopes. They employ automatic rifles, submachine guns, and tommy guns to hunt their game. Some of the Arabs stalk the Arabian Oryx to prove their manhood. They believe that killing an Oryx will give them its "legendary courage and virility." Other poachers hunt for profit. As Henderson points out, a pair of Oryx on the open market may bring a price of thirty thousand dollars.

LYNN HEIDEMANN

Documentation: Footnotes

In a long formal paper, footnotes are the practical way of giving credit to a reference. Footnotes allow the reader to proceed smoothly through the paper without interruption if he so chooses, but permit the more studious reader to stop and study the credits at will. Unlike the bibliography, the footnote is more than a mere list of sources used. It furnishes the reader actual information from the source in the form of a quotation, a summary, or paraphrase, and supplies all the information required should the reader want to locate the book or article in the library or order it from the publisher. Footnotes are for the benefit of the reader and must be written with this in mind so that they clearly communicate detailed, specific documentation to him.

College students use three types of footnotes:

1. Footnotes that cite the exact location of borrowed material.
2. Footnotes that provide explanatory statements to clarify material in the text.
3. Footnotes that refer the reader to another source containing more information.

Of course, no set rule governs the needs of all research papers. At times you will need to combine these forms.

Footnotes are familiar to every reader although some readers consistently ignore them. If you will think about it, however, you will realize how much you already know about the form used to write them. Since the footnote is written for the reader's convenience, there are a number of established conventions to assure uniformity. As with bibliography citations, the large variety of materials requires numerous forms.

Note the following rules for arranging the information within the citations:

1. Indent five spaces and place a raised Arabic number corresponding to the one used in the text.

2. Cite the author's full name in regular order followed by a comma.

3. Enclose the title of an article in quotation marks; underline the title of a book.

4. For a book give publication data consisting of city, publishing company, date, page number. For a magazine give name of magazine, with or without volume number, date, and page number or numbers.

In your research you will encounter scores of books, articles, journals, and indexes. Some will prove valuable to you; others will be of little value. The valuable sources will appear in your paper more than once and will require citing in more than one footnote. To duplicate a full footnote each time a book is cited is a waste of time. In these instances, the first footnote for the book or article, called the *primary* footnote, provides full information about the author, the title, and the publication of the work. A later footnote about the same work—the *secondary* footnote—needs to provide only a short identification of the work. Note: Where printers italicize, students should underline.

A primary citation for a book:

[2] Erich Von Daniken, *Chariots of the Gods* (New York: Bantam Books, 1968), p. 10.

Would become a secondary citation:

[3] Von Daniken, p. 12.

or

[3] Von Daniken, *Chariots*, p. 12.

If you have used more than one book by the same author such as Von Daniken's *Chariots of the Gods* and *Gold of the Gods*, you must use a short title to identify which of the author's books is being cited.

[3] Von Daniken, *Chariots*, p. 22.

[4] Von Daniken, *Gold*, p. 8.

Another measure designed to avoid duplication is the use of *Ibid.* This Latin word, meaning "located in the same place," is used only when a footnote refers to the same source cited directly above it. It is always capitalized, because it is the first word in the citation; underlined to indicate it is a foreign word; and always followed by a period since it is an abbreviation. *Ibid.* alone is acceptable if the page number is identical to that of the preceding footnote. *Ibid.*, plus page number is used if the page number differs.

> ³ *Ibid.*, p. 13.

After a magazine article has been cited once in a footnote, use an abbreviated secondary form for any subsequent references to it. A secondary footnote should include the last name of the author if given, the name of the magazine underlined, and the page number.

> Primary citation for a magazine:
> ⁴ "The Latest Teen Drug: Alcohol," *Newsweek*, 5 March 1973, p. 68.
> Secondary citation:
> ⁵ *Newsweek*, p. 69.

If more than one article is cited from *Newsweek*, the date should be given.

> ⁶ *Newsweek*, 5 March 1973, p. 68.

> Primary citation for magazine with author:
> ⁷ Hope Ryden, "Goodbye to the Wild Horse," *Reader's Digest*, 98 (May 1971), 228.
> Secondary citation:
> ⁸ Ryden, *Reader's Digest*, p. 228.

Footnotes are placed at the bottom of the page on which the notes appear. Regardless of their complexity for the writer, footnotes should be convenient for the reader, providing him with immediate information of where the material may be found without his searching through the paper. However, a popular trend is to place footnotes in a list at the end of the paper rather than at the bottom of each page. Notes placed at the end of the paper are referred to as Endnotes or References Cited. Wherever footnotes appear, however, they are numbered consecutively throughout the entire paper and utilize primary and secondary citation forms. Endnotes should be placed on a separate page *after* the last page of the text and *before* the bibliography page.

A list of footnotes should be set up as follows:

1. Triple space between the last line of text and the first footnote.
2. Indent the first line of the footnote five spaces; the second line should be flush with the left-hand margin.
3. Single space within the footnote, and double space between notes.
4. Footnotes are numbered consecutively throughout the entire paper.

5. Footnotes always list the author's name in normal order, not inverted.

6. Units of information within the footnote are separated by commas or parentheses.

7. A footnote always lists a page number where material may be located.

8. The footnote ends with a period since it is really an abbreviated sentence.

Index to Model Footnote Forms

1. Anonymous Author

[1]"New Outlook for the Aged," *Time*, 2 June 1975, pp. 44–51.

2. Anthology

[2]Michael W. Peplow and Arthur P. Davis, eds., *The New Negro Renaissance: An Anthology* (New York: Holt, Rinehart and Winston, 1975), p. 29.

A single selection from this anthology would read:

[3]James Weldon Johnson, "Fifty Years (1863–1913)" in *The New Negro Renaissance: An Anthology*, eds. Michael W. Peplow and Arthur P. Davis (New York: Holt, Rinehart and Winston, 1975), p. 7.

3. Bible

[4]Genesis 1:3–6.

4. Book
Primary citation:

[3]Maya Angelou, *Gather Together in My Name* (New York: Random House, 1974), p. 2.

Secondary citations:

[4]Angelou, p. 2.

or use a shortened title for easy identification:

[5]Angelou, *Gather Together*, p. 2.

5. Co-authors

[5]Sylvan Barnet and Marcia Stubbs, *Practical Guide to Writing* (Boston: Little, Brown, 1975), p. 26.

6. Double Reference
When you find material from one book quoted in a book you are using, you have two options. You may name either your source or the original if information on the original can be found. Credit may also be given in the text to simplify the reference.

[7]Shirley Graham DuBois, *His Day Is Marching On* (Philadelphia: J. B. Lippincott, 1971), p. 28 quoting W. E. B. DuBois, *The Crises*, October 1926, p. 15.

[8]W. E. B. DuBois, *The Crises*, October 1926, p. 15, quoted in Shirley Graham Dubois, *His Day Is Marching On* (Philadelphia: J. B. Lippincott, 1971), p. 28.

7. Editor

[10]Henry Cabot Lodge, ed., *History of Nations* (New York: Collier Press, 1913), p. 30.

8. Encyclopedia

[9]"Pyramids," *World Book Encyclopedia* (1970), XV, 810–11.

9. Government Document

[3]U.S. Department of Labor, *Occupational Outlook Handbook 1974–75 Edition* (Washington, D.C.: U.S. Government Printing Office, 1974), p. 223.

10. Graphic Materials
Borrowed maps, charts, graphs, diagrams should be given credit in a citation directly beneath the graphic material instead of in a footnote. No reference number is used.

Reproduced from *The World Book Atlas* (Chicago: Field Enterprises Corporation, 1966), p. 119.

11. Informational Note
Informational notes may take any form necessary to convey information. They should be reserved for information that is needed to clarify the material discussed in the text.

12. Interview

[6]Mohammed Ali, Personal Interview, Phoenix, Arizona, 6 April 1975.

13. Magazines
Primary citation for magazine excluding volume number:

[4]Harvey Arden, "In Search of Moses," *National Geographic,* January 1976, p. 3.

Primary citation with volume number:

⁵Harvey Arden, "In Search of Moses," *National Geographic,* 149 (January 1976), 3.

Secondary forms:

⁶Arden, p. 3.

or

⁷Arden, *National Geographic,* p. 3.

Primary form using military style of dating for a weekly publication.

⁸"Crime and Punishment," *Time,* 26 April 1976, p. 82.

Secondary forms:

⁹*Time,* p. 82.

If more than one article is cited from *Time,* the date of issue should be given.

¹⁰*Time,* 26 April 1976, p. 82.

14. Multiple Authors
Works with three or more authors may be listed under the major author's name with the phrase "and others."

⁷Stephen Dunning and others, *Reflections on a Gift of Watermelon Pickle* (Glenview: Scott, Foresman and Company, 1966), p. 143.

15. Multiple Volumes

⁴Milton Rugoff, ed., *The Great Travelers,* Vol. 2 (New York: Simon & Schuster, 1960), p. 661.

16. Newspapers

⁷Conrad Jensen, "Phoenician Backpacks into Lofty Himalayas," *Arizona Republic,* 8 June 1975, Sec. A, p. 1.
⁶*Arizona Republic,* Phoenix, 8 June 1975, p. 10.

17. Pamphlets

⁹*Take Off Pounds Sensibly* (Chicago: n.p., n.d.), p. 2.

18. Split Note

A work may be identified in full or in part in the body of the paper. In this case, the information might be split, with some information given in the text and the remaining information cited in a note at the bottom of the page. The information cited in the text need not be repeated.

19. Unpublished Manuscript

Follow the primary form for a book as close as possible, although some information may be missing. When necessary, identify the source in parenthesis.

[6]Jane E. Welder, "A Study of Black Poetry" (Master's thesis, 1949), p. 12.

20. Untitled Article

[9]*Essence*, August 1975, p. 2.

EXERCISE I	Match each citation in the left-hand column with the appropriate description.

_____1. Jones, p. 12.

    A. Secondary footnote citation for a book (title not indicated).

_____2. *Ibid.*

    B. Consecutive secondary footnote citation (different page).

_____3. *Ibid.*, p. 10.

    C. Footnote citation from the same book, same page.

_____4. Jones, *Earning*, p. 12.

    D. Bibliography citation for a book.

_____5. Von Daniken, Erich. *Gold of the Gods.* Boston: Putnam, 1973.

    E. Secondary footnote citation for a magazine.

_____6. Cooney, John D. "Egypt's Pyramids." *Science*, September 1961, pp. 60–68.

    F. Primary footnote citation for a magazine with an author.

_____7. Erich Von Daniken, *Chariots of the Gods* (New York: Bantam Books, 1968), p. 10.

    G. Bibliography citation for a magazine.

_____8. John Florescu, "A Night in Dracula's Castle," *Seventeen,* January 1974, p. 36.

    H. Secondary citation for a book with shortened title.

_____9. Florescu, *Seventeen*, p. 37.

    I. Primary footnote citation for a book.

_____10. "New Outlook for the Aged," *Time*, 2 June 1975, p. 45.

    J. Primary footnote citation for a magazine without an author.

Indicate whether each of the following is single spaced or double spaced: **EXERCISE II**

_____1. The spacing between footnotes.

_____2. The spacing within a footnote.

_____3. The spacing within the text of a research paper.

_____4. The spacing within a bibliography citation.

_____5. The spacing between bibliography citations.

Identify the traits of a *bibliography* citation by placing a "B" on the line, and the traits of a *footnote* by placing an "F" on the line. **EXERCISE III**

_____1. Author's last name is first.

_____2. The first line is indented five spaces.

_____3. The list is alphabetically arranged.

_____4. The list is numerically arranged.

_____5. Second line is indented five spaces.

_____6. Author's name appears in regular order.

_____7. Specific page number is present.

_____8. All pages of article are given.

Answers to Exercises

III		II		I	
1.	B	1.	Double	1.	A
2.	F	2.	Single	2.	C
3.	B	3.	Double	3.	B
4.	F	4.	Single	4.	H
5.	B	5.	Double	5.	D
6.	F			6.	G
7.	F			7.	I
8.	B			8.	F
				9.	E
				10.	J

49

The Thesis Statement

Writing should not take place until you have limited your chosen subject, decided what you are going to say about the subject, and arranged the order in which you are going to discuss the main points. Then the subject and what you are going to say about it should be clearly stated in a single sentence called the *thesis statement*. The thesis statement sets forth the main point of your paper. However, it should be more than just an announcement of a broad general topic; it must present a specific, limited statement of what you intend to say. The thesis statement is the most important sentence in your paper. In structure it is no different from any other sentence in that it contains a subject area, which announces the subject, and a predicate area, which announces what you are going to say about the subject.

Illegal immigrants

(*Subject*)

have created problems for United States citizens

(*Predicate*)

The need for careful framing of the thesis cannot be ignored since this sentence must clearly communicate the whole purpose for writing the paper. Writers must not confuse or hold the reader in suspense. Beginning writers sometimes neglect to frame the thesis, hoping to stumble upon the reason as they write. They fail to realize that effective writing requires a target, a destination at which the writer wishes to arrive by the end of the paper. The reader should know clearly and precisely what he is reading about or he may not want to pursue it. A reader, like a traveler about to embark upon a trip, deserves to know where he is going. If you cannot state the basic idea of your essay in a single sentence, you probably have not narrowed your subject sufficiently or you have not clearly formulated your objective.

After you have read extensively about your subject, you will find that you have developed interests in certain areas more than others. These interests narrow your subject and become the focus of your paper. Include them in constructing an informal purpose statement before framing the thesis. For example:

> My purpose in writing this paper is to show that alcoholism is increasing among teenagers because alcohol is easy to obtain. It is also very addictive and has parental acceptance over drugs.

This could result in a thesis statement:

Alcoholism

(Subject)

is becoming a problem with American youth

(Predicate)

The writer of a short paper must be aware that he has limited time and space to discuss the problem. Therefore, he may wish to spell out specifically what areas he intends to develop. This spelling out may be thought of as a blueprint or an ordering of the major ideas to be discussed. Adding the following blueprint to the subject and predicate informs the reader of the direction the discussion will take.

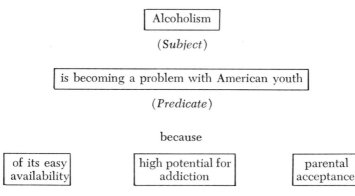

Alcoholism

(Subject)

is becoming a problem with American youth

(Predicate)

because

of its easy availability	high potential for addiction	parental acceptance

(Order of blueprint ideas to be discussed)

Another example of a purpose statement is the following:

> My main purpose in writing this paper is to discuss the founding of the Department of Health, Education, and Welfare in 1953 and to discuss the major role it has played in promoting the social welfare of Americans through Social Security.

The resulting thesis containing a blueprint of the main ideas might be:

> Since the Department of Health, Education, and Welfare was established in 1953, it has indeed promoted the general welfare in the areas of health, education, and Social Security.

Diagrammed, the main ideas would look like this:

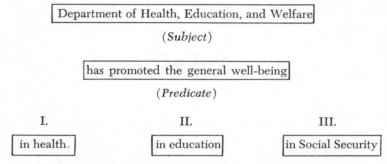

Department of Health, Education, and Welfare

(*Subject*)

has promoted the general well-being

(*Predicate*)

I.	II.	III.
in health.	in education	in Social Security

(*Ordering of the major blueprint ideas to be discussed*)

Now the reader knows what the subject is, what is going to be said about the subject, and in what order the major ideas are going to be presented. The ordering of ideas is also a start in planning the arrangement of the outline you will need to prepare before you write your paper. When writing the outline and the paper, discuss the main ideas in the same order as they are arranged in the blueprint. Be sure that the major ideas are of equal significance to achieve a sense of balance. Discussing your most important or strongest idea last builds a climax and allows you to leave the reader with a sense of fulfillment.

Never make your thesis a question! After all, *you* are writing the paper; it is you who have done the research. It is unfair to ask the reader to answer for you. Almost without exception a question can be converted into an acceptable thesis by writing the answer. For example:

> *Question:* What is responsible for the rising crime rate?

> *Thesis:* The rising crime rate can be attributed to increasing population in cities, rising unemployment, and growth in drug usage.

THE MAJOR IDEAS IN THE BLUEPRINT	become	THE MAJOR DIVISIONS IN THE OUTLINE

Department of Health, Education, and Welfare

plus

has prompted the general well-being

☐ ☐ ☐
Subject + *Predicate* + *Blueprint*

becomes — THESIS: The Department of Health, Education, and Welfare has promoted the general well-being in health, education, and Social Security.

Major Idea I

in health

becomes — I. Before the formation of the Department of Health, Education, and Welfare, fulfilling health needs presented a major problem for Americans.
A. (Supporting material
B. to develop Major
C. Division I.)

Major Idea II

in education

becomes — II. The Department of Health, Education, and Welfare contributes money, advice, and knowledge to the improvement of American education.
A. (Supporting material
B. to develop Major
C. Division II.)

Major Idea III

in Social Security

becomes — III. Most of all, the Department of Health, Education, and Welfare improves the lives of millions of Americans through the Social Security Administration.
A. (Supporting material
B. to develop Major
C. Division III.)

Restatement of the thesis — *becomes* CONCLUSION

Of course you have read numerous articles that start with questions, but you should wait until you are practiced enough with establishing a thesis before you resort to this technique. Without skill, it becomes nothing more than a beginner's clumsy way of getting started.

Remember to establish your thesis clearly and concisely in one sentence early in your paper, usually as the last sentence in the introductory paragraph. Then follow a logical and direct course in supporting the thesis, and you and the reader can end up together—on target.

After your thesis has been clearly established with a subject, a predicate, and a blueprint, you may feel it lacks "sparkle." Students also want their thesis statements to reflect polish and professionalism. This polish might be obtained in two ways:

1. Through the use of vivid word choices.
2. Through the use of lively and varied sentence patterns.

One student writing on alcoholism had framed her thesis statement in this way:

> Alcoholism is becoming a problem with American youth because of its easy availability, advertising, and parental acceptance.

She felt that while the sentence clearly communicated her purpose, it failed to express the severity or magnitude of the problem. She decided to analyze her word choices to determine whether or not other words might better serve her purpose. This was the result:

> Alcoholism is *increasing at a staggering rate* among young Americans because of its easy availability, *seductive* advertising, and parental acceptance.

Adding more vivid words helped to convey a greater sense of urgency about alcoholism, but the sentence pattern was still basic and elementary. A change in the sentence pattern might permit omission of the colorless verb "is," which contributed little to the meaning, and the phrase "because of," which added bulk. At least four choices of sentence patterns might have helped accomplish her purpose:

SENTENCE PATTERN	REFINEMENTS
1. Reduce wordiness by exchanging the verb "is" for a more active, lively verb: "increases."	Alcoholism *increases* at a staggering rate among American youth because of its easy availability, seductive advertising, and parental acceptance.
2. Vary the sentence pattern by introducing a phrase defining the subject or adding explanatory information.	Alcoholism, *a disease affecting four hundred thousand American teenagers*, increases at a staggering rate because of easy availability, seductive advertising, and parental acceptance.
3. Distinguish between major and minor ideas by creating subordinate clauses or phrases.	*Although recognized as a grave disease*, alcoholism increases at an alarming rate because of its easy availability, seductive advertising, and parental acceptance.

4. Invert the sentence presenting the blueprint first.	*Easy availability, seductive advertising, and parental acceptance* contribute to the alarming increase in alcoholism among American youth.

Since the thesis is the single most important sentence in your paper, it deserves thoughtful attention. State your thesis clearly early in the paper. Do not be afraid to experiment with sentence patterns. Write your thesis statement five or more ways and select the pattern which specifically and vividly presents your ideas.

From the following purpose statements formulate a possible thesis. Remember, a thesis is *one sentence only!*   ExERCISE I

    1. The purpose of this paper is to investigate the problems which arise from using credit cards and to show how the average consumer often misuses them, and ends up in bankruptcy or other financial problems.

_____   _____   _____

    Subject   Predicate   Order of ideas
                                              discussed

Now write the final thesis in a smooth, well-worded sentence.

_____

_____

    2. My purpose is to show how educational programs such as "Sesame Street" and "The Electric Company" can help young children to learn. I want to show some of the skills taught such as the use of numbers and the alphabet. Children are also introduced to many experiences they would not see in their own worlds in a colorful, enjoyable way.

_____   _____   _____

    Subject   Predicate   Order of ideas
                                              discussed

_____

    3. My purpose is to show the reader that suicide is increasing at a shocking rate in the United States today, especially among young adults, teenagers, and even very young children.

Subject	Predicate	Order of ideas discussed

4. My purpose is to explain what caused the disappearance of the inhabitants of Mesa Verde through presenting the three leading theories that attempt to clarify the mystery. Some archeologists believe that they left because of extended drought; some that they wished to avoid invading tribes; and some that a plague devastated their tribe.

Subject	Predicate	Order of ideas discussed

The Outline

Many students admit to notoriously bad habits in outlining. What appears to be the typical student's approach to outlining is to write the paper from memory and then write down an outline that agrees with the paper. Yet we expect engineers to build our bridges from carefully constructed blueprints, pilots to fly airplanes by safely charted routes, and chefs to serve food from time-tested recipes. It is logical then to suspect that writers also require direction. Like a blueprint, a map, or a recipe, an outline provides that direction.

When you are writing a research paper, a carefully planned outline can help you to present your subject in an orderly, logical sequence. Skipping from subject to subject loses a reader quickly. A well-arranged outline can facilitate reader comprehension because it establishes a logical thought pattern. In reality, however, the outline is of greatest importance to the writer for it permits him to arrange the ideas to be discussed, to decide the most logical sequence of those ideas, and to establish the major divisions of the material. Of course your outline may require changes as you proceed: an addition here, an elimination there, or a switch in order of presentation. These alterations are acceptable, for the outline should be flexible.

Outlining is not an isolated step in research writing. You have already begun the outlining process when you record notes from your readings on note cards. You outline further when you add captions or labels to the note cards and sort the cards with similar labels together. These captions may become the major points discussed in your paper. Following is an illustration showing how a student researching the conquest of Mount Everest progressed from the informal outline taken from note-card labels to a purpose statement, a thesis, and finally to a formal sentence outline. The major divisions of the outline support the thesis and reflect the structure of the completed paper.

The list below represents the labels on all of the student's note-cards. Brackets indicate material containing similar information. Given broad subject labels, these groups form the major divisions of the paper.

History and Background of Himalayas
{
Name of mountain
Namesake
Mapping of Himalayas
First opened to European climbers in 1920
First attempt
The Sherpas—people who live there
People
}

The Route and Supplies
{
Description of preparations
Porter's pay
Sherpas
Rocks and equipment
Equipment transported
Acclimatized
Food
Liquid intake
}

The Early Attempts to Climb Everest
{
Second reconnaissance, 1922
"English Air"
George Leigh Mallory
1933 attempt
Other failure
North face before World War II
Southern aspect of mountain
Politics and war
Great Crevasse
Spring 1952
}

The British Team
{
Camp I
Description of Iafall
Camp II
Camp III
Neighboring mounts
Team effort
Leapfrog Operation
Last night before ascent
Bad start in May 1953
Clothing time
}

The Success
{
On the top
Description of Hillary
Description of Tenzing
Death of Sherpas
}

With the knowledge derived from the research material recorded on her notecards, the student had enough information for five major points:

1) Description of the early attempts to climb Everest
2) The successful conquest of Everest
3) Background and history of the Himalayas
4) Description of the British team's climb
5) The route and supplies needed

Ready to formulate a thesis, she decided to write a purpose statement as a means of getting started.

> My purpose is to give the history and background of the conquest of Mount Everest, the world's highest mountain located in the Himalayas.

The conquest by a British team led by Edmund Hillary, a New Zealander, and Norgay Tenzing, a Sherpa, took place on May 29, 1953. Since I was impressed by the large numbers of people who had tried to conquer Everest throughout the years, I would like to acknowledge their efforts.

This purpose statement was transferred into the following thesis:

Everest was not subdued by the two men who ascended to its summit on May 29, 1953, but over a period of thirty-two years and by hundreds of men.

The student decided that the main points should be organized in this sequence, moving from the earliest history to the successful climb.

I. Background and history of the Himalayas
II. Description of the early attempts to climb Everest
III. The route and supplies needed
IV. Description of the British team's climb
V. The successful conquest of Everest

The student then converted these five main topics into carefully worded sentences and arranged the supporting information from the notecards under each appropriate heading. This conversion resulted in a final formal sentence outline from which the student could work with little need for change in content. Later, transitions were added for coherence; sentences were polished, and the final formal outline headed by the thesis was typed to accompany the paper. The finished outline reflects the smoothness of thought, unity of content, and order of ideas that comes with careful planning. See this outline accompanying the sample paper on Everest later in this book.

The outline process is designed to show the order, the unity, and the relative importance of the parts of the research paper. For consistency, certain conventional practices have been developed. The outline symbols used most commonly are:

I. Roman numerals represent major divisions of the paper.
II.
    A. Capital letters indicate supporting ideas for the major divisions.
    B.
        1. Lower Arabic numbers and lower case letters show minor de-
        2. tails. Thus the outline works in descending order from most important to least.
          a.
          b.

Writing full scale outlines, however, may be frustrating for the beginning writer. The mechanics of placing the ideas with the appropriate symbol is often confusing in itself. Therefore, beginning researchers may find it helpful to use an outline which summarizes the paragraphs to be written in the paper. In this type of outline it is necessary to use only two divisional symbols, Roman numerals to represent the major divisions or topic sentence of the paragraph, and capital letters to indicate the supporting points which will be used to develop the topic sentence.

I.

    A.
    B.
    C.

Outlines can be written in several forms, using phrases, using topics, or using full sentences. The full sentence paragraph outline has been used throughout this book since it is especially suited for the relatively short research papers assigned herein. In a sentence outline every item should be a complete sentence. The sample paper "Help for the Child Abuser" later in this book provides further information on how the paragraph outline is used in the finished paper. Some advantages to using a full sentence outline are that:

1. Ideas can be completely and clearly expressed.

2. Full sentences can be understood more clearly than a single word or phrase.

3. The sentence, well thought out and well-constructed, may be transferred directly to the text of the paper eliminating the need for rewriting.

4. Full sentences are understandable even if time elapses between the constructing of the outline and the writing of the paper.

The following two-step outline states the thesis sentence then utilizes complete sentences to outline *one* paragraph from a 500 word theme.

THE TWO-STEP OUTLINE

Thesis: Air pollution caused by industries, automobiles, and cigarette smokers is threatening our clean air.

This entire section represents one paragraph

Topic sentence of the paragraph

Supporting points for the topic sentence

I. Major industrial pollutants must be considered first because they are most obvious.

    A. The major contributors include smelters and steel, cement, and chemical industries.

    B. Perhaps as much as three-fourths of industrial dust comes from the burning of fuels.

    C. Gaseous wastes also emanate from industry.

Only the *major* subdivisions of each paragraph should appear in the paragraph outline. While you will be tempted to load your outline with minor details because they are so obvious, resist this urge. Numerous subdivisions may indicate you are including insignificant details or need to add another major division.

You might simplify the outlining process by asking yourself:

1. What are the logical main headings spelled out in my thesis statement?

2. What points from my research notes can be used to develop these main points?

Analyze the following outline of a 500 word essay. Note how the major divisions represent the topic sentences of paragraphs and work to prove and support the thesis. Then read major point I. and so on through the outline and observe how A, B, C and D work to develop and support that paragraph.

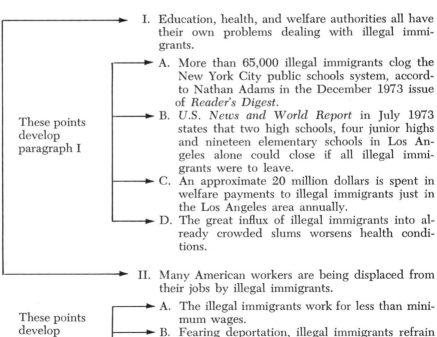

Illegal immigrants create three major problems for United States citizens: in social services, in job displacement, and in increased taxes.

These major divisions are the topic sentences of paragraphs which develop and support the thesis.

These points develop paragraph I

 I. Education, health, and welfare authorities all have their own problems dealing with illegal immigrants.

 A. More than 65,000 illegal immigrants clog the New York City public schools system, according to Nathan Adams in the December 1973 issue of *Reader's Digest.*

 B. *U.S. News and World Report* in July 1973 states that two high schools, four junior highs and nineteen elementary schools in Los Angeles alone could close if all illegal immigrants were to leave.

 C. An approximate 20 million dollars is spent in welfare payments to illegal immigrants just in the Los Angeles area annually.

 D. The great influx of illegal immigrants into already crowded slums worsens health conditions.

These points develop paragraph II

 II. Many American workers are being displaced from their jobs by illegal immigrants.

 A. The illegal immigrants work for less than minimum wages.

 B. Fearing deportation, illegal immigrants refrain from complaining about working conditions.

 C. Mr. Adams avers that an approximate 10.4 billion dollars income is lost by displaced American workers.

III. Illegal immigrants increase taxes for United States citizens.

These major divisions are the topic sentences of paragraphs which develop and support the thesis.

These points develop paragraph III

A. Illegal immigrants receiving welfare assistance cause taxes to rise.

B. Large numbers of illegal immigrants receive government paid medical care.

C. Organizations that handle aliens must be expanded and the money that they use to expand comes from U.S. taxpayers.

D. Deportation stations need increased work forces to handle the greater numbers of illegal immigrants, and the money that pays their salaries is obtained through higher taxes.

Conclusion:

Restatement of the thesis

American citizens suffering from social problems, job displacement, and increased taxes because of illegal immigrants may feel the price is too high to pay.

Remember that when you construct an outline you must adhere to some basic rules. Two major requirements are to arrange the divisions in an effective sequence and to classify the material into logical divisions.

Arranging the order of items in an outline can often be determined by the subject. Most subjects will suggest a natural, logical order, but at times the writer must work to establish an effective order. Some common arrangements are (1) Chronological, (2) Spatial, and (3) Climactic.

1. A chronological order based upon time is easy for a reader to follow and is appropriate for handling discussions of events or processes.

2. A spatial order based upon the relationships in space east to west, left to right is especially effective with descriptive materials.

3. A climactic arrangement enables the writer to move from the weakest to the strongest ideas

Another important requirement in writing outlines is to establish logical relationships. To ensure logical classification within an outline remember three principles:

1. Any series of headings of like rank should be of parallel grammatical structure:

I. Everest's history and background include adventure and heartbreak.	*not*	I. History and background.
II. The early attempts met with frustration.		II. The early attempts met with frustration.
III. The successful attempt took place in 1953.		III. About the successful attempt in 1953.

2. Main headings should not conflict. Categories should be distinct areas which do not overlap:

<table>
<tr><td>

I. In August, 1955, the murder of Emmett Till reflected racial tensions in Sumner, Mississippi.

II. The trial was brief.

III. The acquittal of the accused was swift.

IV. The consequences left their imprint on the killers, Mississippi, and the nation.

</td><td>*not*</td><td>

I. In August, 1955, the murder of Emmett Till reflected racial tensions in Sumner, Mississippi.

II. The trial was brief and the verdict was predictable.

III. The acquittal of the accused could be foreseen, but the results were unexpected.

IV. The consequences left their imprint on the killers, Mississippi, and the nation.

</td></tr>
</table>

3. The subdivision under any heading should logically relate to that heading:

I. Everest's history and background include adventure and heartbreak.

<table>
<tr><td>

A. It was determined in 1852 that Everest was the tallest mountain on earth.

B. Cartographers did not map this area.

</td><td>*not*</td><td>

A. In 1953, the British team achieved success.

B. Cartographers did not map this area.

</td></tr>
</table>

The human mind demands order. If the writer sends the message clearly and coherently, the reader receives the message with understanding. An outline can be the instrument to ensure that result.

The following is a scrambled outline, with a thesis, four major divisions and a list of supporting ideas.   EXERCISE I

1. Identify the four major divisions.
2. Arrange the major divisions in the order that you feel best represents the thesis.
3. Locate the supporting ideas for each of the four major divisions.
4. Arrange the supporting ideas in the most logical order to reflect the thesis.

OUTLINE
TARZAN OF THE APES

Thesis: Tarzan of the Apes, a folk hero of the twentieth century, is one of the best loved characters of fiction because of his superhuman physical abilities, his superior intelligence, and his leadership ability.

The Major Divisions (Organize in the order suggested by the thesis statement using Roman numerals.)

_____1. Tarzan had the characteristics of a leader.

_____2. Tarzan as a literary character has gained immense popularity since his creation in 1912.

_____3. The ape-man also had a very level head and was graced with a superior mind.

_____4. Tarzan's physical abilities are far superior to those of any other human.

Supporting Ideas   (Decide what major divisions the ideas belong to, then organize the ideas in order, numbering them A, B, C.)

_____1. The character has inspired comics and movies, as well as television and radio productions.

_____2. Finally, Lord Greystoke was a perfect example of masculine beauty.

_____3. The Tarzan books are filled with adventure and excitement.

_____4. In addition, he knew more about the jungle than did any other human.

_____5. Tarzan's adventures represent the daydreams all men have.

_____6. He first became king of his tribe of apes.

_____7. He later became chief of a tribe of warriors.

_____8. First, the ape-man possessed strength and agility far beyond that of the normal man.

_____9. Most of all he was extremely ingenious and was seldom outwitted.

_____10. He had a well-developed memory and was quite well educated.

_____11. Next, Tarzan's reflexes were far more developed than those of civilized man.

_____12. He later claimed his due as Lord Greystoke, an English nobleman.

_____13. Third, Tarzan did not age like other men.

_____14. The Tarzan character has been popular in best-selling hard books and paperback books.

Answers to scrambled outline for "Tarzan of the Apes."

	10. III A	5. I D
14. I B	9. III C	4. III B	2. II
13. II C	8. II A	3. I C	3. III
12. IV C	7. IV B	2. II D	2. I
11. II B	6. IV A	1. I A	1. IV

In some cases, the arrangement of the subpoints (A, B, C, D) under the major divisions (I, II, III, IV) may depend upon the preference of the writer.

Suggestions for Producing a Readable Paper

When you reach the writing stage in the development of your paper, you have already worked many hours in searching for materials in the library, in preliminary, broad, general reading, in narrowing your subject, in taking notes, in formulating the thesis, in arranging the note cards, in developing the outline. Now you are ready to present your findings to others. In addition to this accumulation of research materials, remember that your years of experience, your attitudes and memories, and your ways of expressing yourself are important resources from which to draw. This paper is yours. It displays *your* creativity. It should not be dull or uninspired; it should represent you at your best. It should be a paper that could not have been written by anyone else, because no one else has lived the same life you have, has thought all of your thoughts, or has had all of your experiences.

THE INTRODUCTION

For many students, writing the introduction is the most difficult part of the process, but this beginning is fundamental to a successful paper. A good introduction enables the writer to gain the attention of readers, to stimulate their interest, and to evoke attitudes that will hold their attention throughout the paper. The introduction should make people want to read the paper. It should relate the subject directly to the readers' personal interests and it should help readers to understand what you are saying.

The introduction allows you to set forth your purpose and point of view, to define your terms if necessary. It provides an opportunity to limit the topic, survey the background, state the proposition, and announce the divisions of the paper.

An introduction should be balanced with the rest of the paper. A long, rambling introduction defeats its purpose and consumes valuable time needed for development of the body of the paper. Too short an introduction may fail to make the reader receptive to what follows. The introduction should not distract from the subject. Rather, it should smoothly and logically move into the thesis statement which is the main point of the paper. *The thesis statement should be the concluding sentence of the introductory paragraph.*

Introductions defy rigid classification. They are a matter of personal preference. Every paper, however, requires an introduction fitted to the reader, the writer, and especially the subject. These five types seem to be most common:

1. Personal reference.
2. Anecdote.
3. Pronouncement.
4. Description.
5. Background.

Each of these types provides an effective lead-in to a research paper. The following brief discussions suggest why and when each will be most effective. The sample introductions were all written by students of Mesa Community College: *

1. *Personal Reference.* This type of introduction attempts to establish a common bond between writer and reader. It is appropriately used when the writer determines that his readers will have shared his anxiety about a problem, his memories of persons, places, or things. It says to the reader, "We are not strangers. We have concerns in common."

PRISON REFORM

Our prisons have failed. Crime increases daily. Millions of man hours and billions of dollars are spent yearly to depress this crime rate, but to no avail. According to Raymond K. Procunier, Director of the Cali-

---

* The footnote citations from the original student papers are not reprinted in this text.

fornia Department of Corrections, "Out of every one hundred inmates released, thirty-six will make it on the outside without any problem. Thirty-nine have questionable adjustment; that is, they don't come back to prison, but they're in and out of county jails, stealing a little over here, using some dope over there—they're staying at the local level. Twenty-five come back to state prisons almost immediately."[1] In other words, thirty-six out of one hundred really make it. If we are to improve prison conditions, we must reform our idea of prisons, increase public awareness, and rid ourselves of racial problems associated with prison bureaucracy.

Daryl L. Price

THE CREDIT CARD DILEMMA

There used to be stores in the rural parts of America that the present generation has recently become familiar with because of television shows like "The Waltons" and "Little House on the Prairie." I suppose the first credit card was used in a rural store. It probably was a brown paper bag on which the proprietor wrote purchases and payments. Those casual business dealings have accelerated into "the big card game of our plastic society," as P. O'Neil referred to the credit card business in a recent *Life* article.[1] The big card game, the multiplicity of credit cards, has caused endless problems for businesses and consumers through unwise distribution and use.

Becky Tucker

2. *Anecdote.* An anecdote need not be humorous, although it may be. It may be a dramatic true story, or even a quiet, simple incident from everyday life. Pertinent and well-told stories attract the interest of individuals of all ages. The common response to a lively or dramatic story helps to establish rapport between writer and reader.

Four year old Andy Larson loved to explore his parents' bedroom. It was filled with such exciting objects. Although his mother kept the door closed, Andy had learned to climb on a hall table and open it. Today was a good day for exploring; his mother was talking on the telephone. He opened the door, dashed for the big bed, and jumped joyously up and down three times. He fell laughing into the huge pillow. The slightly opened drawer of the bedside table caught his attention. Pulling the drawer wider, he saw a big black 38 caliber revolver. "Bang, bang," he cried pointing the gun around the room. "Bang!" it responded as the trigger tripped. That shot echoes throughout this country hundreds of times a year as defenseless children fall victim to the careless storage of lethal weapons. Improved gun control laws are needed to end loss of life caused by accidental shootings, to limit the use of guns for violent crimes, and to decrease the power of pro-gun lobbyists.

Luella Smart

THE MYSTERY OF VAMPIRES

In June 1918, Mrs. Hayes took a small house in Penlee, South Devon. She wrote: "I had a friend staying with me, but otherwise we were quite alone in the place. One morning we came down to find in the middle of the parquet floor of the sitting room the mark of a single cloven hoof in mud. The house and windows were very small, so it was quite impossible for an animal to have gotten in. We hunted everywhere for a second trace but without success. For several nights I had most unpleasant and frightening experiences with an invisible but perfectly tangible being. I had no peace until I hung the place with garlic, which acted like a charm. I tried it as a last resource."[1] This is just one of the many stories which involve vampires. Although cases of vampirism may be rare, occult phenomena, they do exist, but are often hushed up.

MARY FRANCES SANCHEZ

3. *Pronouncement.* Beginning writers sometimes fail to realize that the best way to begin a paper is often simply to begin. That is, they may start the paper with a statement about the subject. They may use facts or figures—startling ones can be effective here. They may use a quotation or cite an opinion expressed about the subject.

ALCOHOLISM: A YOUTH PROBLEM

Presently some 450,000 teenage alcoholics reside in the United States. Seventy-five percent of all high school students are regular drinkers, and more than one-half of that percentage have a serious drinking problem. These startling facts, reported in the March 1974 issue of *Seventeen*, p. 10, remind us of one of the most widespread, most destructive problems in our country—teenage alcoholism. Why has alcoholism become such a problem among the youth of our country? Some answers to this question can be readily observed: there is a rising trend towards alcohol use instead of drug abuse; there is an increased availability or opportunity to obtain alcohol; and many youths turn to alcohol to solve their personal problems.

DWIGHT W. CORRIVEAU

THE PYRAMIDS OF EGYPT AND CENTRAL AMERICA

Modern-day businessmen have manufactured small scale pyramids for purposes ranging from sharpening razor blades, dehydrating flowers, and mummifying eggs to promising the need for fewer hours sleep by those persons sleeping in six-foot vinyl ones. These mass-produced, commercial items are truly a debasing contrast to the masterpieces of skill and engineering of the pyramids of Egypt and Central America. The pyramids contain the finest masonry of the world together with inner secrets revealing ancient cultures that may have even surpassed the intelligence and knowledge archeologists and scholars give them credit for.

BARBARA C. KANO

WHAT HAPPENED TO AMELIA EARHART?

"I have a feeling that there is just about one good flight left in my system, and I hope this is it. Anyway, when I have finished this job, I mean to give up major long distance flights." Amelia Earhart made those statements before she left on her incompleted flight around the world in 1937.[1] The strange disappearance of Amelia Earhart caused many unsettled feelings. Nobody could answer the question with certainty of what had happened to her. Today, thirty-eight years later, the same question still remains unanswered. According to the Navy Department, Amelia Earhart's plane crashed and was lost at sea, but research and new discoveries have kept the Earhart mystery alive.

JORI WRIGHT

4. *Description.* Setting the stage for the reader by appealing to his senses of sight, hearing, touch, taste, and smell can establish his mood or cause him to experience a sensuous or emotional awareness of the subject. While an effective descriptive introduction may require skill in using words, most individuals are capable of describing some memorable event, location, or emotion.

OPERATION DEEPFREEZE

Colorful mountains rise like tombstones over the wind-rippled snow. Stormy ice-choked seas swirl against the desolate land. A faint sun reflects its colors off the frigid blue ice. This is Antarctica, a cruel land tormented by icy storms and chilling temperatures. This is the environment the men working on operation deepfreeze lived in for months and sometimes years. But their time and effort proved valuable because the outcome of operation deepfreeze had a significant effect in promoting scientific research, forming an international organization, and increasing goodwill in the nations that participated.

RAMONA SMITH

THE MYSTERIOUS CONTINENT
OF ATLANTIS

The sky was filled with billowy clouds of black smoke. Huge eruptions of fire and molten lava rocketed into the air and floated to the ground. The earth shook with every thundering explosion from the volcano. In one single day and night, some 10,000 years ago, the continent of Atlantis sank into the ocean to become a mystery to all. Before the catastrophic eruption, this island of Atlantis was known to be an abundant land. Plato located it in the Azores. People and cultures surrounding the area confirmed his theory of location.

HENRY MILLER

THE VALUES OF CHILDREN'S PROGRAMS

A tangled mass of legs is seen behind a confusion of shoe bottoms. On the sole of each shoe is printed a letter of the alphabet. A chaotic movement of twisting legs and flying shoes suddenly begins. Order emerges from the mess. The word "picture" is formed with the letters. As fast as the last word is contrived, another word is made by the swinging of shoes on bending legs. Does this description bring a strange scene to your mind? What is actually going on is learning. Second, third, and fourth graders tune the television to the children's program "The Electric Company" daily. Programs like "Sesame Street" and "The Electric Company" provide children with a means of learning simple facts, being shown what they can do for themselves, and, above all, being stimulated to learn.

CYNTHIA LINNAE

5. *Background.* The introduction can supply the reader with information he needs to understand what follows. It may place the subject in its historical, cultural, or social setting. It may briefly survey what has been commonly accepted as a valid position, then lead the reader into exploring a new one.

THE GROWTH OF THE POLIO VACCINE

Although other communicable diseases strike more persons each year, few have such drastic and lasting effects as polio. No part of the world is free from it, and it may occur as an epidemic or in scattered places. Polio did not receive serious attention until an epidemic broke out in Sweden in 1887. Epidemics of polio became prominent in the United States after the beginning of the 20th century, with the highest number ever recorded being 57,890 cases in 1952.[1] Something had to be done to stop these polio epidemics. Three major stages in the development of a polio vaccine were the use of gamma globulin, Cox's vaccine, and Salk's vaccine.

JORI WRIGHT

FILLING THE GAP

The generation gap of today did not suddenly flair into existence, but began in the early development of the family structure. This lack of understanding between parents and their children can be compared to an electrical spark and the way it is produced. To produce this spark, or misunderstanding, two conductors are needed. To close the gap between parents and children a better understanding must come about so that communication between the two can flow easily with little or no resistance. This process of communication is left up to the parents and how they train their children. Filling the gap and strengthening the relationships in the family will begin when parents teach their children, while they are young, the proper methods of communication, respect, and justice.

LARRY BARNES

SUEZ: LIFELINE CUT

The year 1956 was memorable in many ways. This was the year that the first transatlantic telephone cable was laid, the year of the Hungarian revolt, and the reelection of President Eisenhower. One of the most startling of the happenings of this year, for the Western powers, was the seizing and nationalization of the Suez Canal by Egypt. The action came, President Nasser said, because aid from the United States, France, and Britain for the Aswan High Dam on the River Nile was cut off. This action by Egypt created three major problems for the Western nations.

MARK NICHOLS

Following these suggestions will help you to write effective introductions. Be creative, too; rely on your own ingenuity.

THE CONCLUSION

Remember Alice's conversation with the Cheshire Cat in *Alice in Wonderland?* Alice asked the Cat:

"Would you tell me, please, which way I ought to go from here?"

"That depends a good deal on where you want to get to," said the Cat.

"I don't much care where . . . ," said Alice.

"Then it doesn't matter which way you go," said the Cat.

". . . so long as I get somewhere," Alice added as an explanation.

"Oh, you're sure to do that," said the Cat, "if you only walk long enough."

After reading the introduction written by other students, you should realize that it does matter what course you set your paper on if you hope to arrive at a destination of understanding and acceptance from your reader. And having reached somewhere, you must convince your reader of that fact. The conclusion should do this convincing. Your research paper should *end*, not just *stop*. Your reader should not be left hanging in mid-idea. A conclusion need not be long nor involved, but it should leave the reader satisfied that the writer has said what he had to say, not just run out of words or gone out for lunch.

The conclusion is the final chance for the writer to say, "Look, I've said something of importance, so pay attention" or "Now that you understand there is a problem, this is what you can do about it." It is the last opportunity for the writer to restate and emphasize the main idea of his paper. In the conclusion, the writer may become philosophical, suggesting the importance of his ideas to humanity. He may end with an apt quotation or well-stated comment by an authority.

The following are conclusions of several of the papers from which the introductions were taken. See if you can determine which endings go with which beginnings:

More research has been done on children's programs than on any others on television. More questions have been asked about them, and many have not been answered yet. However, the question "Are they educationally sound?" has been answered with a definite "Yes." What children can gain from watching programs like "Sesame Street" and "The Electric Company" has only begun to show itself; but we do know that these programs are more valuable than anyone ever expected them to be, and, as they continue, they will teach children in new and vital ways.

Title of Paper: _____

Written by: _____

Is our society forcing young people to drink to be accepted? Perhaps. We have lowered the drinking age, making it easier for youth to obtain alcohol; we have "billed" alcohol as something desirable, and have said alcohol is legal while other drugs are not. Previous generations as well as the present "adult" generation have established a deadly pattern—a drinking norm—for America's youth to follow. Milton Wolk of the Massachusetts Department of Health and Alcoholism declared: "Teenagers have always used alcohol and they always will. And because teenage use is patterned after adult use, there's no way kids are going to stop drinking until adults do."[9]

Title of Paper: _____

Written by: _____

These problems must be faced by all the Western countries that are affected by the Suez Canal's seizure. If response to our predicament is not immediate, we could well find ourselves grinding to a halt without the oil that industries need so badly. By seizing and nationalizing the Suez Canal, the Egyptians could put a short-term stranglehold on the world, and, if they do so, the only country that will gain in the long run is the Soviet Union.

Title of Paper: _____

Written by: _____

It is interesting to ponder the idea that these ancient cultures could very well have been even more advanced than we are today. They may have had technologies we have yet to discover; therefore, we are unable to understand them. Another more disconcerting thought concerns the reason for their deterioration. Do technological advancement and superior knowledge mean extermination? Some historians feel we should look to these ancient cultures as a warning. That our present-day technological achievements will, in effect, turn on us and conquer or destroy us may be indicated by all forms of pollution in our water, land, and air. An analogy might be drawn between the massive slave population of Egypt being robot-like under the rule of the mighty kings and the people programmed for specific functions of society in George Orwell's book, *1984.* We should perhaps recognize the danger that exists when power is relagated to a few and delegated to the masses, as surely it must have been when the Pyramids were built, when the Pharaoh played the double role of king and god.

Title of Paper: _____

Written by: _____

An inevitable by-product of operation deepfreeze was the increase of goodwill among the people of the twelve nations working together. This brought about the forming of an international organization called the Special Committee for Antarctic Research. The forming of this international committee seems to be one of the most important outcomes of the time spent at the bases in Antarctica because it proves that people from different countries and different backgrounds can learn about and discuss each other's points of view, as well as work together in peace for a cause that benefits the world and each individual nation.

Title of Paper: _____

Written by: _____

DEVELOPMENTAL PARAGRAPHS

Because the beginning and ending of any research paper form the reader's first and last impressions, effective introductions and well-written conclusions will strengthen your paper. If you look at a diagram of a 900-1,000-word paper, however, something else becomes clear. Examine this diagram and do some mental arithmetic:

Title

Thesis:	Introductory paragraph (125-150 words)

1.	(Approx. 150 words)

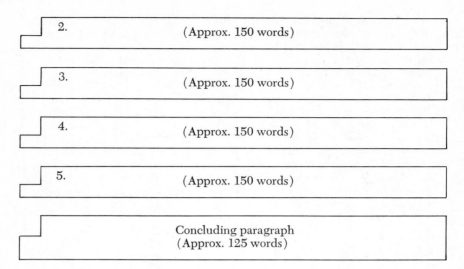

2.	(Approx. 150 words)
3.	(Approx. 150 words)
4.	(Approx. 150 words)
5.	(Approx. 150 words)
	Concluding paragraph (Approx. 125 words)

You can see that at least 750 words (approximately five paragraphs) make up the body of the research paper, so you need to devote proportional time to making these paragraphs informative and readable. They carry the burden of developing your thesis completely and specifically. They must lead your reader to an acceptance, or at least an understanding, of your ideas. They must convince him that you have a thorough knowledge of what you are writing about. In addition, they must keep him reading. A vital, lively introduction promises much. You cannot afford to disappoint your reader in the ensuing paragraphs, or he will feel cheated.

Most rhetorics list several methods of paragraph development, such as use of specific details, use of examples, use of contrast or comparison, use of cause and effect, use of definition, use of narration, use of description. Most paragraphs are not just one of these, but a combination. All well-developed, effective paragraphs have these common qualities:

1. *A controlling idea.* This idea is often placed at the beginning of the paragraph as a topic sentence. Certainly, if you take care that each paragraph you write has a topic sentence, you are likely to produce adequate, perhaps excellent, paragraphs. The topic sentence announces the subject matter of the paragraph and with a key word or two indicates how that subject will be limited or developed in the paragraph.

2. *Unity.* Every sentence in the paragraph should relate to the controlling idea. It should add reasons for and cite examples or facts in support of the main idea of the paragraph. If extraneous matters creep in, then eliminate them, for they will destroy the unity of your paragraphs.

3. *Coherence.* Not only should every sentence relate to the controlling idea, but the reader should understand exactly how it relates. He should never have to puzzle over a statement wondering what on earth it has to do with anything. Through repetition of important words or phrases, synonyms, transitional devices, you glue your paragraph together and enable the reader to move smoothly from one idea to the next.

4. *Logic.* The paragraph should make sense. When you write, you must think; you must reason. You must avoid twisting or exaggerating evidence just to make it fit. You must refrain from making sweeping generalizations which you do not, or cannot, support. You should be wary of using "always," "never," "everybody," "nobody," "everything," "nothing," or "all," unless you can prove the statement.

5. *Adequate development.* A paragraph is not just an idea—that can be stated in a single sentence. A paragraph is a *developed* idea. "I think I will bake a cake for dinner" is an idea, but you cannot eat it. Not until the shortening, sugar, eggs, flour, milk, salt, baking powder, extract have been combined, step by step, not until these ingredients have been put in a pan and baked in an oven heated to the proper temperature are you going to have a dessert. In the same way, a paragraph must be full of facts, dates, names, places, examples, illustrations, and reasons before it is going to be palatable and before it is going to satisfy the appetite of the mind.

Read the following paragraph:

> Building the pyramids took lots of work by many men. Thousands of them had to work many days just to haul the stones, let alone the time spent in building. They had to work day and night just to get the stones to the place of construction. It was a tremendous job.

Now ask yourself, "What have I learned by this paragraph?" Your answer? All most of you can say with any certainty is that building the pyramids took lots of work by lots of men. Not very satisfying, is it? Now look at what one student wrote to impress upon the reader the fact that the work required to build the pyramids was "tremendous."

THE ENIGMA OF THE EGYPTIAN PYRAMIDS

> Herodotus, the ancient Greek historian, when investigating the pyramids, was told by Egyptian temple priests that it took a labor force of one hundred thousand men twenty years of constant drudgery to complete the task of constructing the Great Pyramid. If we were to compute mathematically how many stones it would be possible to put into place daily by the available amount of labor, we could roughly find the amount of time it would take to construct such an object. It has been estimated that the strength of twenty men would have been required to move each ton of weight a mile a day up an inclined plane. The average weight of each of the 2.6 million blocks that constitute the Great Pyramid is approximately 6.25 tons. This information gives us a maximum of eight hundred of those blocks that could be moved a mile a day, as-

suming all of the available work force labored around the clock.[6] Hypothetically, if this were the case, it would have taken approximately nine years just to move the entire weight of the mass one mile. This estimation does not consider the amount of time spent in construction, which would be considerably greater, but only that spent moving all the blocks to the site itself. Clearly, the pyramid could not possibly have been built in twenty years by the means traditionally employed, even with that great a labor force.

LAWRENCE ALLEN HULL

Not content with "lots of men" or "lots of weight" or "lots of work," this student has used specific numbers, one hundred thousand men, 2.6 million blocks, 6.25 tons. Step by step he estimates the time required just to move the blocks. He demonstrates the overwhelming task it was.

Remember that an effective paragraph will have a main idea, unity, coherence, logic, and adequate development. Examine the following paragraphs. Notice how each student has complied with the requirements for satisfactory, readable, informative paragraphs.

In the first two paragraphs the students announce their material by the topic sentence, then fill their paragraphs with names and specific references. In the first example, the word "associates" serves as a key word to the content of the paragraph. In the second, "'key' witnesses" serves this function.

DR. JONAS SALK'S MIRACLE VACCINE

Salk's *associates* during his years of research were an important asset to his discovery. Dr. Tom Francis, for whom Salk was an apprentice, was an integral part of Jonas' early years as a scientist.[10] He gave him the laboratory training and experience that was necessary for Salk's research. Dr. Francis was also one of the few highly ranked microbiologists to believe in a killed-virus vaccine,[11] which became the type Salk developed. Through his friendship with Basil O'Connor, President of the National Foundation for Infantile Paralysis, Salk was able to receive funds for laboratory space and equipment to carry on his research. O'Connor also stood by him during the days of uncertainty and confusion after the vaccine was released.[12]

DAWN LAMBSON

EMMETT LOUIS TILL

The state called a total of twelve witnesses, but only three were considered "*key*" witnesses. It was Robert Hodges, age seventeen, who found Emmett's body. He described the location, and also informed the jurors that a cotton gin fan had been tied to Emmett's neck to weigh down his body.[15] Willie Reed, age eighteen, claimed he saw Emmett and six other men riding in a pickup truck on the morning of the abduction. Later, he testified that he saw the same pickup truck parked by a barn and heard "some licks" and "oh, oh" coming from the inside. Then he stated that he saw Milam carrying a pistol and walking from the barn to the well for a drink.[16] When Mose Wright, Emmett's uncle, was asked if the men who abducted his nephew were present, he stood up fearlessly and pointed a finger at Roy Bryant and J. W. Milam.[17] Emmett's mother, Mrs. Mamie Brandley, gave as her testimonial the positive identification of Emmett's body. She also found the ring given to Emmett by his deceased father, with the inscription LT, on her son's finger.[18] But even with the witnesses and positive identification, the state fought a losing battle.

DEBBIE CLINT

In the following paragraph note how the student developed the idea of the Amazon Indians' experiences with the white men, especially the ideas of cruelty and carnage. Here, unity is achieved by the specifics used in support of the topic sentence. Each sentence supplies additional information: first, of what the experiences had been, and second, of the result.

GO YE AND PREACH THE GOSPEL

The Indians of the Amazon had known a long tale of cruelty and carnage with the white man. Ironically, while Spanish-Catholic missionaries were trying to christianize the infidel tribes, Spanish and Portuguese raiders hunted the brown-skinned people like wild animals and sold them as slaves. Whites came in search of rubber, and brought with them diseases, weapons, machines, and clothes, that had an unhealthy effect on Indians in the hot climate. Because these Indians were a hunting and warring people, males had a high death rate; as a result, women were plentiful, and the Indians saw no fault in polygamy, which the white man forbade. In a controversial article on the incident, "Murder of Five Missionaries," Dr. Stirling, an expert on the Indians of Ecuador, said, "They resented interference with their own religion and the attempt to substitute for it the ideologies completely foreign to their own background and completely incomprehensible to them."[9] It was inevitable that the Indians revolted against the restrictions being put on them. They had their fill of persecution and infection. To survive, the Aushiri Indians adopted a policy of complete isolation that has continued to this day and is enforced unto death. They kill outsiders, then flee into the jungle. For this reason, the Aushiri are named "the Phantom People of the Curaray," because they disappear so effectively and silently.[10]

BRIAN JUDD

As you can see from these examples, paragraphs are developed ideas, complete with specifics, dates, names, illustrations, which support the controlling ideas. In addition, paragraphs maintain coherence by the use of transitional devices. These stratagems carry the reader from what has gone before to what is coming next. They aid him in connecting ideas and in developing relationships. Read the following paragraph aloud. As you do so, emphasize the italicized words and phrases:

SIGNIFICANCE OF THE DEAD SEA SCROLLS

The increased knowledge gained from the Dead Sea Scrolls has given the world a better insight into the background of *Christianity.* Scholar Andre Dupont-Sommer states that the beginning of the *Christian Church* began with the renewal activity of the *Qumran monastery* from 4 B.C. to 68 A.D.[4] The *Qumran texts* reveal the Jewish world as a complex reality. *The Scrolls* show striking *similarities* of expression and ideas with some of the material from the *New Testament. Both* have in common the ideas of human brotherhood and love; *both* preach poverty, humility, and chastity; *both* practice a form of communism. *In both,* the essential rite is a sacred meal, so well known in the Last Supper. *Other points of similarity* are the insistence on temperance and self-control, the belief in the eternal life of the soul, in the coming of the Messiah, and the idea of ritual washing with its typical form of baptism. *In addition,* the term "the Righteous One" applied to the Master of Righteousness in the Manual is matched by the terms applied to Jesus in the Gospels. *Because of these similarities,* it seems probable that many of the *Qumran expressions* became part of the general pattern of thought and served as vehicles for the *New Testament* and early *Christian teachings.*

ESTHER LOPEZ

Through repetition—but not overworked—through parallelism ("both have," "both preach," "both practice"), through phrases ("other points of similarity," "in addition," "because of these similarities"), the student has led the reader from one sentence to the next, carefully guiding him through the comparison.

USE OF QUOTED MATERIAL

Although writing research papers requires all of the basic techniques needed for any effective writing, it also poses some problems of its own. Working facts, statistics, opinions, and quotations supplied by other writers smoothly into your text demands planning and skill. You want to avoid trite, awkward, inept handling of research materials; at the same time, you must acknowledge sources and let your reader know why you are presenting certain information. If you will examine the paragraphs already cited, you will see that these students did work the knowledge they had gained in their research effectively into paragraphs. (In each of these paragraphs, you will notice elevated numbers indicating that the source for the information has been cited in a footnote.)

Skillful use of borrowed materials is essential to writing a readable research paper. In Shakespeare's *Hamlet,* Polonius, the pompous counselor to King Claudius, pontificates:

> Neither a borrower nor a lender be
> For loan oft loses both itself and friend;
> And borrowing dulls the edge of husbandry.

I. iii. 78–81

This advice may be sound when the subject is money, but it cannot be followed implicitly when you are writing a research paper—unless you are working on a completely original project and no one else has contributed anything. There are times when a bit of quoted material adds to the depth and vividness of an idea; it enlarges the reader's perspective and triggers his imagination. Extensive borrowing, however, particularly in the form of quotations, does dull your ingenuity and may substitute for the hard mental effort needed if your paper is going to be uniquely yours.

Observe how the quoted lines in the following paragraph appropriately develop and echo the observation made in the topic sentence:

DRACULA: FACT OR FICTION

Much research has been conducted by Professors Raymond McNally and Radu Florescu of Boston University about the legend of Dracula. They found that his true name was Vlad Tepes and that he was born around 1431. He was a Christian prince, who ruled in what is now Rumania. He took pride in his kingdom's reputation for honesty, and would do anything to keep his people from lying and stealing. "No tyrant of the time could quite compare with him," stated Professor Florescu in referring to Dracula.[1] Professor McNally has been quoted as saying,

> Vlad was trying to rule by terror. . . . Before he came to the throne, Transylvania was a lawless land. During his time, there seems to have been law and order in the streets of his kingdom.[2]

Both professors felt that this reign of terror could be attributed to Vlad Tepes' style of torture and execution.

Cathy Gage

In the following excerpt from a student's paragraph, the bit of quoted material is from the play President Lincoln was watching the night he was assassinated. The writer describes Booth's actions:

MYSTERIES SURROUNDNG THE ASSASSINATION
OF PRESIDENT ABRAHAM LINCOLN

He bored a hole in the doorway that led to the Presidential box—a hole which would serve as a peephole to spy upon the Presidential party that night. He then made a hole in the plaster by the door and jammed a stick into it, thus bracing the door and preventing entry from the hall. Now he was ready. That night during the performance of the comedy *Our American Cousin*, Booth waited patiently by the door, listening for the right line which would signal his attack. Then it came, the heartiest laugh line of the play: "Wal, I guess I know enough to turn you inside out, you sockdologizing old mantrap." Booth entered, aimed the pistol at the back of the laughing President's head, and pulled the trigger. Because of the heavy laughter, few of the audience heard the shot.[3]

DWIGHT W. CORRIVEAU

In the following excerpt, the student quoted some lines from Homer's *Iliad* because accuracy was important:

SCHLIEMANN: THE FINDING OF TROY

Nineteenth-century scholars believed Troy and Homer were myths, but Schliemann believed Homer implicitly. Schliemann found a reference in the twenty-second song of the *Iliad* indicating the location of Troy. Schliemann was particularly interested in lines 145–152, involving a description of two springs running through the Trojan plain: "One of these runs hot water and the steam on all sides of it rises as if from a fire that was burning inside it. But the other in the summertime runs water that is like hail or chill snow or ice that forms from water."[8] Schliemann, using references from Homer, chose Hissarlik instead of Bunarbashi as the site of Troy.

KIM DEON HICKS

The student then went on to describe why Hissarlik was the correct choice.

Sometimes it is next to impossible to summarize what an author has said, or to choose other words that will adequately accomplish what must be accomplished. Observe in the following paragraph the conciseness with which John Cottrell describes the relic believed to be the Holy Grail:

THE LEGENDS OF THE GRAIL

Occasionally a person will set out on his own pilgrimage in search of the Grail. John Cottrell wrote about his quest in the April 1971 issue of *Ladies' Home Journal*. He traced the Grail from Wales to Palestine and with Joseph of Arimathea to Glastonbury. In the sixteenth century the monks fled the Abbey to escape King Henry VIII's war against the Roman Catholics. They left the relic at the House of Namteas in the cave of the Powell family. With the death of the Powells, it went to Mrs. Betty Minylees. The centuries old relic is still in her possession.[15] John

Cottrell saw the relic, thought by many to be the Holy Grail. He described it as a "gnarled wooden object, darkened with age, reduced to one-third its original size by centuries of wear. Originally, it measured about five inches in diameter around the top and three inches in depth, tapering to a ball about two and one-half inches across. Its edges were dented and pitted with teeth marks."[16] There is no scientific proof that the object described is the Holy Grail, but documents kept by its owners show how the cup was bent to cure people and how drinking or eating from it did effect cures.

CYNTHIA LINNAE

Whenever you feel the urge to quote, ask yourself this question: "Why am I quoting this phrase, this sentence, or these sentences?" Your answer will give you either the green light or the stop sign. Quote if you answer:

1. I am citing an authority to clinch a major point I am making in my paper.

2. I am quoting these lines from a poem, a play, or a novel because the author chose them with care and changing them would damage a work of art.

3. I am quoting from this legal document, diary, or letter because I might change the meaning if I summarized.

4. I am quoting because the original is so concise I would use twice as many words if I summarized.

Having decided that quotation is justified, you should follow these steps:

1. Always introduce or in some way lead into a quotation: who said it, where it was said, its importance, etc. The quotation may be integrated as part of your sentence. It may be introduced, "According to . . . ," ". . . said, "The following shows . . ."

2. Once the quoted passage is cited, you should follow with a comment about it, an interpretation of it, a reference to a phrase or word in it. The quotation will then become a part of the fabric of your paper.

3. You must quote exactly. Although you may omit words, or even sentences, and insert an ellipsis (. . .), you may not change any portion of the quotation. Three spaced periods are used if omitted words were internally placed in one sentence. Four spaced periods are used if words omitted include a period at the end of a sentence.

4. Direct quotations of fewer than three lines are usually typed into the text, e.g.:

In Plato's words, the voyager traveling West from Atlantis "had access to the island and from the latter to the opposite continent which is located at the edge of the real ocean."[6]

5. Direct quotations of more than three lines should be indented and single-spaced. Unless the passage is enclosed in quotation marks in the original, it should not be enclosed in quotation marks on your paper. E.g.:

> One of the major puzzles is why the pyramids were constructed. Several theories have been formulated as to their purpose, but not enough solid, convincing facts support any single one. C. W. Ceram, in *Gods, Graves and Scholars*, states:
>
>> The meaning of the pyramids can be grasped only in terms of Egyptian religious beliefs. The urge to build pyramids was rooted in the basic Egyptian belief that after physical death the soul continues to exist through all eternity. . . . this conception of life after death had two related results: the practice of mummification and the construction of fortress-like pyramids.[3]
>
> The conviction that their king was also a deity was so strong that the ancient Egyptians believed he needed three abodes: a tomb, a mortuary temple, and a palace.[4]

Revising

You have already designed the blueprint for your paper by developing a thesis statement and outline. You have completed the major tasks of construction by giving form to the outline with introductory, developmental, and concluding paragraphs. You have indicated what material must be acknowledged with footnotes. Take a deep breath! Perhaps you feel you deserve a rest, but you cannot quit now. You must revise! To reach this point, you have followed some definite steps which have been clearly delineated for you; but the process of revision is so individual and complex that it is difficult to say exactly what you should do or in what order. You have to be a juggler, keeping half a dozen or so balls in the air at a time.

You know that you should write one sentence at a time and avoid sentence fragments, that you should punctuate and spell correctly, that you should make subjects and verbs and nouns and pronouns agree. If you have problems with sentence structure and grammar, consult a complete English handbook. Use your dictionary to verify and correct spelling. There is no acceptable excuse for misspellings.

These are routine matters, but must be attended to. In addition, you should:

1. Read what you have written, see it, hear it, evaluate it.

2. Revise sentences so that they are clear and concise, and so that they flow smoothly from one sentence to another.

3. Evaluate each word, asking: (a) Is this the most accurate, most specific word I can use here? (b) Is this the most vivid, lively word available to convey my meaning?

4. Check for shifts in point of view.

Begin the revising process when you are alert and energetic. Read aloud. Your ear will hear the awkward repetitions in sentences like:

Parents who are abusive to their children often had parents who abused them and so they abuse their children.

or

The pyramids were built by the pyramid builders who built them with lots of work.

Your mind will sense the confusion in:

Increasing crimes by prisoners demand people do something to help them or they will just keep going back to prison.

Often you cannot correct a sentence simply by inserting or deleting a word or two. You must throw away the entire sentence and start fresh:

Today's abusive parents were probably mistreated when they were children.
The pyramid builders moved tons of stones and labored hundreds of years.
Because those released from prison often repeat their crimes, people must work for more effective prisoner rehabilitation programs.

If a sentence, possibly even several sentences, does not read smoothly, if it does not make sense, eliminate it and rewrite the ideas.

REVISION OF SENTENCES

Sentences can be long, short, simple, compound, complex, questions, statements, commands. You have been writing all of these for a number of years, and the process has become pretty much routine. When you are striving for excellence, however, you cannot be content with habitual procedures. You must become conscious of what degree of formality you are striving for and what sense of strength and emphasis. You must determine what pace is best suited to your paper's subject.

Because a research paper is more formal than a personal essay, you should eliminate the following:

1. First-person point of view.
2. Use of contractions.

3. Use of slang and colloquialisms.

4. Informal sentence patterns, either short and elliptical or long and rambling with many asides and interruptions.

Sentence Patterns

In a formal research paper, sentence patterns should be neither breezy nor long-winded, should be neither "Wow! Those pyramids were something else!" nor "Those pyramids now (you know it really took a lot of work to get them together) were built by slave labor, no union pay nor forty hour week in those days—poor slobs." Sentence variety is necessary for readability, but it must be a carefully controlled diversity. If you want your paper to speed up, such as when you are describing an event, then shorten the sentences and strive for action verbs:

> The A-bomb committee *selected* several sites as possible targets. President Truman *chose* Hiroshima and Nagasaki because they were principal industrial and military centers.[7] *Reaching* this decision, he *announced* the news to Japan. Through letters and messages, he *warned* Japan concerning the atom bomb. He *demanded* unconditional surrender or Japan would be bombarded by the most destructive weapon devised. Japan *refused* to surrender.

To achieve a more leisurely pace, lengthen sentences:

QUETZALCOATL, THE FEATHERED SERPENT

> Quetzalcoatl, one of the favorite priest-rulers of Mexico, claimed several names and titles. He was the god of life and fertility, inventor of agricultural processes, patron of arts and industries, and the originator of the calendar and priestly rituals.[3] Men, considered to be the sons of Quetzalcoatl, built effigies of him everywhere in Mexico. Although confusion arose from other persons' use of his religious titles, the important part of his story, whether history or legend, remains that Quetzalcoatl disappeared promising to return again in the year of the Aztec calendar called "Ce Acatl." Because of this promise Montezuma did not attack when Cortez first landed in Mexico. The Aztecs thought the prophecy was coming true and that Cortez, the god, had returned to reclaim his empire.[4]

JOANNE WILLIAMS

Coordination

Sentence structure also contributes to formality. Formal sentence patterns are balanced through coordination. The coordinating words, *and, but, for, or, nor,* connect like grammatical structures: clauses, phrases, nouns, verbs, adjectives, adverbs. The following paragraph contains several balanced constructions.

> Nikita Khrushchev, in the Twentieth Congress of the Communist Party of the Soviet Union, on February 15, 1956, denounced his master *Josef Stalin* and *his policies.* (coordination of nouns) Khrushchev denounced Stalin for *his intolerance, his brutality,* and *his abuse of power.* (coordination of series: nouns as objects of preposition "for") Khrushchev blamed Stalin for *the division of Germany, the institution of slave labor camps in Siberia,* and *the oppression of Russian Satellites.* (coordination of series: nouns as objects of preposition "for") Ironically, the policies that Stalin dictated had been carried out by one of his pupils, Nikita Khrushchev, making him as *brutal* and *intolerant* (coordination of adjectives) as Stalin. Khrushchev *had been close* to Stalin and *always followed* (coordination of verbs) Stalin's policies in every respect. Khrushchev, playing a deceitful game, both *revived* and *attacked* (coordination of verbs) one of Stalin's supporters, the notorious chief of the Secret Police, Lavrenti Beria. People who wished to betray Beria to *Khrushchev* and *the Central Committee* (coordination of nouns: objects of preposition "to") were *shot* without trial and *sentenced* (coordination of verbs) by Beria after execution. Beria's idea was useful, for soon after Stalin's death, Khrushchev had Beria shot and sentenced him later.

Few students have difficulty with coordination when just two elements are joined: men and women, barked and howled, for the people and by the people, the lightning flashed and the thunder cracked. Almost automatically students make these elements parallel, that is, of the same grammatical structure. When three or more elements are linked, however, more effort is needed to keep the grammatical structure identical. Look again at the paragraph on Khrushchev. "For his intolerance, his brutality, and his abuse of power" is a series of coordinate prepositional phrases, with the preposition *for* omitted before the second and third objects. Whenever a sentence branches, remember to make the branches of equal grammatical structure:

The retarded are special people
        who need   *care*
                    training *programs*
                    educational and vocational *guidance*
                    and
                    most of all, *love.*

The archeological wonder of King Tutankhamen's tomb
        was that   *it was* relatively undisturbed
                     it brought to light new facts about Egyptian lifestyles
                     and
                     it clarified many facets of an
                        Egyptian King's burial.

Trading stamps   *brought* more business to stores
                   made the consumer spend more money
                           and
                   caused almost endless problems.

Subordination

Both coordination of sentence elements and subordination contribute to clarity. Both enable the reader to move smoothly from one thought to the next, mentally linking those ideas which must be joined. Subordination especially works to show relationships. The subordinating conjunctions—*when, after, because, while, if, until, where, before, although,* etc.—introduce dependent clauses (ideas that depend upon another clause for their meaning). The relative pronouns, *who, whom, that, which,* also introduce subordinate clauses.

In revising your paper, work for smooth, effective subordination; if sentences seem choppy and unrelated, determine the relationship of ideas and subordinate those of less importance to those dominant ones. Read the following sentences:

The bank card is versatile. It is easily used. Individual and family debts have increased. Americans owed a collective debt of $6.6 billion in 1974.

In this form, these four sentences are simply four ideas with no relationship shown among them. They might be rewritten to read:

Because the bank card is so versatile and easily used, the collective debts of Americans, family and individual, increased to $6.6 billion in 1974.

Sometimes a group of short sentences cannot be efficiently combined into just one sentence. You may need two:

Some banks sent out unsolicited cards. Bad credit risks received cards. The banks had trouble collecting debts. Most banks now send cards that are requested. They check applicants.

Rewritten, they might read like this:

Since many banks at first sent out unsolicited credit cards, they had difficulty collecting from bad credit risks. Today, most banks issue bank cards only after they have checked an applicant's credit rating.

Notice in this rewriting how the main ideas have been placed at the end of the sentences to emphasize their importance.

Relative pronouns introduce adjective clauses: the man *who* works in the bank; the woman *who* manages the hardware store; the expedition *that* was led by Hillary. Although these pronouns are handy words— or perhaps *because* they are handy words—they are frequently overused, with the result that writing becomes heavy with deadwood. The use of relative pronouns should be limited. Most of the time, these clauses can be reduced to phrases, with a resultant tightening of sentence structure and heightening of interest for the reader.

Archeologists *who* have determined approximately when Stonehenge was constructed at first believed *that* it was built by the Druids, *who* were priests of the pagan Celts *who* lived in England.

Rewritten:

Archeologists have determined approximately when Stonehenge was constructed. They believed at first that it was built by the Druids, priests of the pagan Celts of England.

Especially avoid "which" clauses dangling at the ends of sentences:

The people who built Stonehenge left no history, *which* has created a mystery.

A traveling Greek may have been the final architect of Stonehenge *which* has been indicated by the discovery in 1953 of carvings in the sarsen stone. The carvings are of an ax and a knife or sword, *which* were tools *which* were used by the Greeks at that time.

Rewritten:

Because the builders of Stonehenge left no written history, they are shrouded in mystery.

That a traveling Greek may have been the final architect of Stonehenge has been indicated by the discovery in 1953 of carvings in the sarsen stone. The carvings are of an ax and a knife or sword, tools used by the Greeks in the eighth and ninth centuries B.C.

Coordination of like sentence elements, subordination of ideas to those of more importance, elimination of unnecessary "who's and which's" will make your writing more forceful, and certainly more vivid and entertaining for your reader.

When you are writing a paper to be read by someone else, and you want the reader to understand what you are saying, you cannot be as free with meanings as was Humpty Dumpty in *Through the Looking Glass.* Humpty and Alice were discussing the relative merits of birthday and un-birthday presents. Humpty Dumpty concluded:

". . . and that shows that there are three hundred and sixty-four days when you might get un-birthday presents. . . ."

"Certainly," said Alice.

"And only one for birthday presents, you know. There's glory for you!"

"I don't know what you mean by 'glory,'" Alice said.

Humpty Dumpty smiled, contemptuously. "Of course you don't— till I tell you. I mean 'there's a nice knock-down argument for you!'"

"But 'glory' doesn't mean 'a nice knock-down argument,'" Alice objected.

"When I use a word," Humpty Dumpty said, in rather a scornful tone, "it means just what I choose it to mean—neither more nor less."

"The question is," said Alice, "whether you can make words mean so many different things."

"The question is," said Humpty Dumpty, "which is to be master— that's all."

Alice was too much puzzled to say anything; so after a minute Humpty Dumpty began again.

"They've a temper, some of them—particularly verbs: they're the proudest—adjectives you can do anything with, but not verbs—however, I can manage the whole lot of them! Impenetrability! That's what I say!"

Charged Words

Humpty Dumpty does make a valid suggestion. We do attach meanings to words above and beyond their literal translations. These meanings are determined by our experiences and our attitudes. Therefore, when you write you must be aware of the connotations, the nuances of words. You must work to get the response that you desire from the reader. Examine these lists:

A	B	C	D	E
thin	fat	drunk	nice	cheap
skinny	plump	intoxicated	pleasing	inexpensive
slender	stout	inebriated	agreeable	low-priced
slim	obese	tipsy	enjoyable	reasonable
frail	chubby	high	precise	economical
puny	corpulent	soused	delicate	
scrawny	overweight	smashed	fine	
lanky		polluted	sensitive	
		mellow	critical	
			squeamish	

In each group are words to which we react favorably, words to which we react negatively, and words to which we are neutral. Test yourself to determine which of the words you regard as favorable, which negative: after each word, put a plus for a positive reaction and a minus for a negative one.

Overused Words

Some words have been used so frequently and so indiscriminantly that they have become almost nonwords; they may have no more meaning than a grunt. You should eliminate the following words from any of your sentences and substitute more precise ones. After each word, write a more precise term:

neat _____	item _____
nice _____	deal or great deal _____
great _____	good _____
interesting _____	field or field of _____
beautiful _____	pretty _____
aspect _____	fantastic _____
many _____	very _____
a lot _____	super _____
various _____	some kind of _____
thing or things _____	varied _____

These words are not indispensable. The English language has over half a million words in its vocabulary. Surely you can avoid these few in your writing. Possibly *thing* is the most overworked of them all. What can you use in sentences instead of *thing?*

There are many *things* children learn from children's programs.

Rewritten:

Children learn numbers, the alphabet, meanings of words, love, kindness, and brotherhood from "Sesame Street."

Many *things* were found in the tomb.

Rewritten:

Gold necklaces, intricately carved ivory bracelets, gold-plated chariots, bejeweled coffins, and alabaster bowls were found in Tutankhamen's tomb.

You are really doing yourself a service by removing the word *things.* Being specific enables you to add, in these two sentences, more than twenty words in place of two. If you have difficulty in achieving a five hundred or thousand word requirement, be specific and you will have words to spare. But, more important, you add information, and your reader will be grateful. He grows weary of every action, person, and place being described as "great," or every object, attitude, or idea as a "thing."

Effective Verbs

Humpty Dumpty's comment that verbs have a temper and pride indicates their importance. One of the most reliable ways to improve the readability of your writing is to improve the quality of the verbs. Two methods for enriching verbs are:

1. Change passive voice to active whenever possible.
2. Eliminate bland verbs whenever possible.

Change passive voice to active. In active voice the subject does the action expressed in the verb:

> Plato placed Atlantis "beyond the pillars of Hercules" in the Atlantic Ocean.

In the passive voice the subject receives the action of the verb:

> Atlantis was placed "beyond the pillars of Hercules" by Plato.

In most sentences, you can change the passive voice to active with little effort. Make the doer of the action the subject of the sentence. What you have written then becomes more immediate, more filled with life and movement.

Eliminate bland verbs. Bland verbs lack color; they have no smell or taste; they just sit. The most overused verbs are the whole paradigm of "to be." When you rely too heavily upon them, they drain the life from your writing. Not all of the *is*'s, *are*'s, *was*'s, and *were*'s can be dropped, but hundreds of them can be. At least you should make the effort.

Read this passage describing the removal of mummy wrappings from Tutankhamen's body:

> There *were* many layers of mummy wrappings. The Pharaoh's body *was* decorated with gold and jewelry. Necklaces *were* of gold and

semiprecious stones; rings *were* also of gold and *were* decorated with stones. Tiny gold sheaths *were* on his fingernails and toenails. Around his body *were* heavy gold plaques. On these plaques *were* welcoming speeches by gods and goddesses to the young King as he *came* to the underworld to join his fellow deities. To the Egyptians, the Pharaoh *was* the son of Ra. Ra *was* the god of the sun. On the Pharaoh's death, he *went* to join the gods.

Bland, colorless verbs abound in this paragraph. It shows no excitement of discovery. Such a passage demands revision. A possibility is:

Layers of mummy wrappings *surrounded* the Pharaoh's body. Gold and jewelry *decorated* each layer. Necklaces and rings of gold and semiprecious stones *encircled* his neck and fingers. Tiny gold sheaths *adorned* his fingernails and toenails. Around his body heavy gold plaques *bore* speeches by gods and goddesses as they *welcomed* the young King to the underworld, the realm of his fellow deities. The Egyptians *honored* their Pharaoh as the son of Ra, the god of the sun. At the King's death he *journeyed* to be with the other gods.

The verbs now are in active voice and depict motion.

Verbs combined with their subjects form the core of the sentence; they supply vigor and force; they create pictures; they transport the reader from one idea to the next. Surely words capable of performing all of these tasks must be chosen with care. One of your problems in selecting a verb lies in the depth of choice. For example, think of all the ways to describe movement from one place to the next:

ran	sauntered	marched
walked	crawled	hiked
hopped	crept	stepped
skipped	strolled	scurried
jumped	rambled	hastened
ambled	traveled	

How then do you choose? Imagine the scene you wish to describe. Who is moving? Where? How? Once the picture is set, select the word that abstracts it, that will best enable your reader to recreate in his mind the action you created in yours.

SHIFTS IN POINT OF VIEW

Every time you write, you assume an attitude toward your material. In a personal narrative, describing or explaining an event in your life, you of necessity become the focus of attention and you employ the first-person pronoun frequently: "*I* slammed the door and ran." "As a child,

I lost myself in daydreams." "The circus, a fantasy world, engulfed *me*." Intimately and immediately bound to these experiences, you establish a closeness with your reader by personal references.

In explaining or telling someone how to play the guitar, embroider a shirt, or plant a rosebush, you direct the process of explanation directly to your reader: "Before planting the rose, *you* must prepare the ground." "The design *you* choose for your shirt will determine the degree of artistry *you* achieve." The second-person *you* should be reserved for direct address or appeal to the reader.

When writing about persons other than yourself, about places, contemporary problems, or historical events, you should use third person:

> During a *child's* pre-school years, *he* watches television an average of twenty hours a week.

> *Thor Heyerdahl* explains in his book *The Ra Expeditions* that before Columbus, the *Egyptians* made explorations along the African coast in *their* reed boats.

> The Mesa Verde *Indians* came to America nearly 25,000 years ago from *their* Asiatic homelands. *They* roved and hunted throughout the Southwest.

Because a research paper is formal and because the writer should maintain a certain objectivity, these papers should be written in the third person. During the revision process, you should eliminate any shifts in point of view. Observe what happens in the following paragraph:

> In an urge to escape reality, the alcoholic turns to the bottle. Pressured by what *he* views as a hostile family and an uncaring world, *he* seeks oblivion in alcohol. The young housewife, sick of the routine of *her* life, searches for solace in gin. *You* drink more and more because drinking only increases the problems. If *you* are a teenager confronted with emotional problems, *you* regard drinking as grown up, an escape from adolescent confusion. *I* may drink because *my* parents drink alcohol but will not accept drugs.

In this paragraph, formality and especially objectivity have been lost. The student began with the alcoholic (third person) and moved to the housewife (third person). Then confusion! *You* (second person) shifts to teenager (third person) and on to *I* (first person). By the time the reader approaches "but will not accept drugs," he may be convinced that *he* has had too much to drink.

A revised version, maintaining a consistent point of view, would read:

In an urge to escape reality, the alcoholic turns to the bottle. Pressured by what he views as a hostile family and an uncaring world, he seeks oblivion in alcohol. The young housewife, sick of the routine of her life, searches for solace in gin. She drinks more and more, because drinking only increases her problems. The teenager, confronted with emotional problems, regards drinking as grown up, an escape from adolescent confusion. Although his parents will not accept drugs, they sanction the use of alcohol because they use it themselves.

Maintaining a consistent third-person point of view throughout your paper focuses sharp attention on its subject matter. Thus, the reader's attention will also be concentrated.

These suggestions for making your papers readable by no means exhaust the possibilities. They may, however, stimulate your creative capabilities; they may offer you some tangible means for revision. Trust your own senses and mind; give them an opportunity to work for you. The result is worth the effort. Alexander Pope in his *Essay on Criticism* noted the importance and value of careful writing:

> But true Expression, like th' unchanging Sun,
> Clears, and improves whate'er it shines upon,
> It gilds all objects, but it alters none.
> Expression is the dress of thought, and still
> Appears more decent, as more suitable;
> A vile conceit in pompous words expressed,
> Is like a clown in regal purple dressed.

Practice

Assignment:

First Research Paper

Will Rogers said, "All I know is just what I read in the papers." Millions of Americans also depend upon newspapers, magazines, and television to keep them informed of the current events of this rapidly moving world. They expect these media to provide accurate, reliable, and factual information about people, places, events, and activities. To do this, newspapers must be able to convince the reader that the information is credible and factual. This proof is written into articles:

- According to the fire department, the fire claimed five lives and caused $50,000 worth of damage.
- "The picnic will be held at 2 P.M. in Encanto Park," announced Jane Holmes, Chairman of the Children's Welfare Committee.
- Chief Lawrence Green stated, "The suspect was interrogated for two hours, then released."

These references are forms of in-text documentation, the most familiar means of conveying credit.

The following current topics lend themselves to in-text documentation. Be sure to include names of experts, titles of articles, names of magazines, dates, and pages where the information can be found. *The Reader's Guide to Periodical Literature* and specialized indexes such as

Education Index will help locate articles in current magazines and periodicals. Local and national newspapers provide discussion on the topics. Pamphlets or interviews with authorities also contribute valuable information. The current nature of the topics requires recently published works. Therefore, for this assignment, magazines or periodicals should be used as they provide the most up-to-date information.

Instructions:

1. Select one of the questions from the accompanying list.

2. Locate and read *three* articles or similar sources relating to the subject chosen.

3. Make a bibliography card for each article according to accepted forms. Have bibliography cards checked.

4. Record any information you desire to use in your paper on 4″ × 6″ note cards according to form. Have note cards checked.

5. Arrive at an answer to the question you have chosen based on the articles and your own thinking.

6. Develop a thesis and sentence outline. Have your outline approved by the instructor. Note: Your thesis must *answer* the question. The thesis may not *be* a question.

7. Write a 500–600 word paper, with bibliography, based upon the outline and materials. The paper "Help for the Child Abuser" on page 101 serves as a model for this assignment.

8. Use in-text documentation when citing material from articles. (Do not use footnotes.)

9. Papers should be typed.

10. Fasten completed work in a binder.

Schedule:

1. Check bibliography and note cards: _____

2. Check thesis and outline: _____

3. Paper due: _____

Finished paper must include:

1. Title page.
2. Thesis and sentence outline.
3. Text, accurately documented with in-text documentation.
4. Bibliography.
5. Bibliography cards and note cards, arranged in the order used in the text.

Questions:

1. Why do many children have difficulty learning to read?

2. What are the values for children in programs like "Sesame Street," "Mr. Rogers," and "The Electric Company"?

3. What can be done to make physical education programs more effective in our high schools?

4. What measures should be taken to improve prison conditions?

5. What educational programs may be formed to aid retarded children in developing skills?

6. Why has alcoholism become such a problem in our country?

7. How may alcoholics be helped?

8. How are older people victimized by con artists?

9. What problems have credit cards created for people?

10. What should be done to prevent illegal immigrants from entering the U.S.?

11. What problems do illegal immigrants create for U.S. citizens?

12. What contributes to the increasing rate of suicide among young people?

13. How can a contributor to a charity determine whether or not his money is being spent appropriately?

14. What injustices exist in the lack of uniform sentencing for criminal acts?

15. What changes need to be made, or have been made, in recruiting practices for collegiate athletics?

16. What can be done to increase the availability of vocational programs in our secondary schools?

17. What can be done to improve the quality of parent-child relationships?

18. How may the revising of court procedures improve the criminal justice system?

19. What measures must be taken to protect endangered wildlife? Select one species.

20. What problems are created by the growing rate of illiteracy in the U.S.?

21. What has contributed to the current rate of college writing deficiencies?

22. What are the arguments for (or against) gun control?

23. To what can the rising rates for medical malpractice insurance be attributed?

24. What are the arguments for (or against) the "death with dignity" philosophy?

25. What problems are associated with nursing homes across the country?

26. What services are available to protect the consumer?

27. What effects have Vietnamese immigrants had upon America?

28. What can be done to improve the quality of television programs for children?

29. What are the benefits (or disadvantages) of government subsidies for the fine arts?

30. How have the contributions of certain ethnic groups enriched American society? (Choose one group.)

31. What are the purposes of Affirmative Action plans in government and industry?

32. What are the arguments for (or against) the Equal Rights Amendment?

33. What created the need for the Supreme Court ruling on busing to achieve racial balance in education?

34. What plans have been suggested as alternatives to our present welfare system?

35. What advantages (or disadvantages) does our current welfare system have for the recipient of welfare payments?

36. What improvements have handicapped citizens experienced as a result of changing attitudes toward them?

37. What damage does illiteracy impose upon a society?

38. What is being done or what should be done to help American minority groups participate more fully in higher education?

EXERCISE I

Now that you have observed the use of in-text documentation in your first research paper, you should be able to see how it provides information and establishes reliability to the writer's material. These in-text citations can be easily converted into footnotes for a longer paper.

Locate each in-text documentation cited in the sample paper on "Child Abuse," following this section.

1. What is the author's name?
2. What is the title of the article or book?
3. What magazine published the article? If a book, where, when, and by whom was it published?
4. In what issue does the magazine article appear?
5. On what page does the information appear?

Arrange this information in an acceptable footnote citation. Indent, punctuate, space correctly, and indicate the proper numbering for each footnote.

EXERCISE II

When you receive your first research paper back from your instructor, convert all in-text references to proper footnote citations and record them in acceptable form in the lower margins of your paper.

The following sample research paper was produced by a student in response to the first research assignment. Read it carefully. Note the use of in-text citation as a means of conveying credit to sources used in compiling the paper. Also pay special attention to how the outline works into the paper.

HELP FOR THE CHILD ABUSER

A Term Paper
Submitted in Partial Fulfillment of the
Course Requirements for
English-102
Section 2622

by

Kim Deon Hicks
6 February 1976

Outline

Thesis Statement: Parents who abuse their children can be helped
through private therapy, social service agencies,
and special action groups.

I.   Private therapy, although it is one of the least publicized forms
of therapy used in child abuse cases, is a way for parents to understand themselves, their children, and their problems.

        A. Private therapy is often expensive.

        B. Psychiatrists use group therapy sessions
composed of people with similar problems
as a means of reducing cost of therapy.

        C. Private therapy is important for those
prominent citizens who have an image to
uphold in society.

II.   Social workers and the agencies they work for have contributed much
toward helping child abusers in slum areas.

        A. Social workers counsel the family and
teach them how to show love to
their abused child.

        B. Child abusers are more apt to bring their
battered child to a social service clinic
than to a large hospital.

        C. Social workers who work in slum areas are
able to instill trust in the parents they
are trying to help.

III. Special action groups, aimed at helping both parent and child, are being established in many of the major cities in the United States.

    A. Groups like Mothers Anonymous are formed by ex-abusers who want to help others.

    B. Many American universities are using their Medical facilities to develop new approaches on child abuse.

<u>Concluding Statement</u>: Parents who abuse their children are able to find help and understanding through the numerous services now available.

Steve Samuels was enraged because his eighteen-month-old son Michael *Introductory*
paragraph
had just torn a psychedelic pop art poster. The father seized Michael,

hanged him by the wrists with an electrical cord, and beat him against

the wall for nearly thirty minutes. Michael's mother finally got the infant

to a hospital; he died minutes later of multiple fractures and bruises.

This incident is one of thousands happening every day. Parents, as well as

their children, need aid. <u>Parents who abuse their children can be helped</u> *Thesis*
statement
<u>through private therapy, social service agencies, and special action groups</u>.

<u>Private therapy, although it is one of the least publicized forms of</u> *Major*
division I
<u>therapy used in child abuse cases, is a way for parents to understand them-</u>

<u>selves, their children, and their problems</u>. (A) <u>Private therapy, however, is</u> *Supporting*
point I-A
<u>expensive</u> and everyone cannot afford the hourly rate of a qualified

psychiatrist. As a result, (B) <u>psychiatrists group sessions composed of</u> *Supporting*
point I-B
<u>people with similar problems as a means of reducing cost of therapy</u>. The

combination of group therapy and individual therapy permits treatment of a

maximum number of abusive parents. Even if parents can afford private

counseling, child abuse cases are too numerous for private psychiatrists

to handle all of them. In New York last year, according to an article

"Help for Child Beaters" in <u>Newsweek</u>, 24 July 1972, p. 66, over seven *In-text*
citation
thousand cases of child abuse were reported, and experts estimate that one

child is killed each week by drug-addicted parents. This number does not

cover actual child abuse cases in the United States because most go unre-

ported. Private therapy is accessible to many child abusers, who come from

every race and from every social and economic level. (C) <u>However, private therapy</u> *Supporting*
point I-C
<u>is most important for and most accessible to prominent citizens who have an</u>

<u>image to uphold in society.</u>

Social workers and the agencies they work for have contributed much *Major division II*
toward helping child abusers in slum areas. "Shelter, Children's Center,"
an article in New Yorker, 5 July 1969, p. 21, reports that social workers, *In-text citation*
many of whom live in the area where they are employed, earn the confidence
of child abusers as well as potential child abusers. (A) Social workers *Supporting point II-A*
counsel the family and teach them how to show love to their abused
child and how to welcome that child back into the family group. Until
the worker feels that the abused child will be safe at home, the child is
placed in a special center where his needs are met. These centers often
include clinics staffed with highly-trained volunteer doctors. Neighborhood agencies are especially effective in finding out which parents injure
their children because (B) child abusers are more apt to bring their children *Supporting point II-B*
to a neighborhood social service clinic than to a large hospital. At the
clinic, the counselors try to help parents and child with their problems.
Through kindness and a caring attitude, (C) social workers in slum *Supporting point II-C*
areas are able to instill trust in the parents they are trying to help.
These low-income people are more inclined to trust a neighbor and often
that neighbor is a social worker.

Special action groups, aimed at helping both parent and child, are *Major division III*
being established in many of the major cities in the United States. (A)
Groups like Mothers Anonymous, formed by ex-abusers, want to assist others. *Supporting point III-A*
Phyllis Zauner in "Mothers Anonymous," written for McCall's, January 1972, *In-text citation*
p. 57, discusses the group started by Mrs. Jolly Kajaka in 1970 as an
organization for mothers unable to secure help any other way. Mrs. Kajaka
developed a new form of therapy she describes as layman's reality therapy.

2

She says, "We don't let people just moan about how they were beaten when they were three; we say, 'You're thirty-three now; the problem is to stop doing what you're doing to your children.'" The success of Mothers' Anonymous has spread from California to New York, where the group is called Parents' Anonymous. (B) Many American universities employ their medical facilities to *Supporting point III-B* develop new approaches aimed at eradicating child abuse. The University of Colorado Medical Center has established an approach called "parent aides." Lay assistants, people between the ages of twenty-four and sixty, act as guardians for the parents of battered children. They visit the families and pay no attention to the children, but listen with interest to the parents' problems. They provide a means for parents to work out their frustrations and anger and to achieve an understanding and acceptance of themselves. Once these goals are accomplished, abusive parents no longer need to strike out at their children.

Helping parents who beat, burn, and starve their children is no *Conclusion* simple matter. The complications are many. Through the love and guidance of psychiatrists, social workers, and special groups, some of these parents find comfort and receive understanding. Once they solve their problems, they can strive for a loving relationship with their children.

B I B L I O G R A P H Y

"Help for Child Beaters." <u>Newsweek</u>, 80 (24 July 1972), 66.

"Shelter, Children's Center Deluged With Child Abuse Cases."
    <u>New Yorker</u>, 45 (5 July 1969), 21-22.

Zauner, Phyllis. "Mothers Anonymous: The Last Resort."
    <u>McCall's</u>, 99 (January 1972), 57.

Assignment:

Second Research Paper

One of the steps in gaining maturity is the realization that significant events occurred before your birth. You may even be impressed with the magnitude of those happenings if you roam through "old" newspapers, magazines, and books in search of newsworthy topics. Examine issues of *Life, Newsweek, Time, U.S. News and World Report,* and the *New York Times Index* for the year you were born. Look for events receiving national or international attention in more than one publication. Almanacs, encyclopedias, and yearbooks for that year may also furnish subjects. Digging into the past may prove valuable in understanding the present.

The paper "The Humbling of Everest" is one student's response to an event occurring in 1953, the year she was born.

Subject: Event of national or international importance occurring in year you were born; it may have happened in any state or in any country.

Length: 1200–1400 words, approximately eight typewritten pages (double spaced).

Requirements:

1. At least *six* sources must be consulted and used in the paper.

2. There should be at least *ten* footnotes; each of the six sources must be used at least once.

3. Provide a bibliography card for each source, and a note card for each footnote citation.

4. The thesis, besides indicating the event, should focus on one particular significance of the event: social, cultural, economic, academic, military, person or persons involved, group or segment of population affected.

5. The introduction should specifically state the year researched.

Completed paper should include:

1. Title page.
2. Thesis and sentence outline.
3. Text, documented with footnotes at bottom of page.
4. Bibliography.
5. Bibliography cards and note cards (arranged in order used in the paper). (All should be firmly enclosed in a binder.)

Schedule:

1. Subject chosen: _____

2. Bibliography and note cards checked: _____

3. Thesis and sentence outline checked: _____

4. Paper completed: _____

The following sample research paper was produced by a student in response to the second assignment. Read it carefully and answer the questions that follow it.

THE HUMBLING OF EVEREST

A Term Paper
Submitted in Partial Fulfillment of the
Course Requirements for
English-102
Section 2622

by

Becky L. Tucker
25 March 1976

The Humbling of Everest

Thesis Statement: Mt. Everest was not subdued by the two men who reached its summit on 29 May 1953, but over a period of thirty-two years and by hundreds of men.

I. Although it was determined in 1852 that Everest was the tallest mountain on earth, the impulse to scale its heights was restrained because of superstition and misinformation.

    A. Its location was remote.

    B. The governments and people of Tibet and Nepal distrusted outsiders.

    C. Cartographers did not map this area.

II. Eventually, Tibet opened the way for Europeans to explore Mt. Everest.

    A. The first attempt, in 1921, failed.

    B. The second reconnaissance, in 1922, improved its plans by employing Sherpas.

    C. The 1922 attempt failed as did several other attempts.

III. The Chinese invaded Tibet during World War II and closed the northern route, but Nepal opened the southern route.

    A. Nepal placed restrictions on the number of attempts that could be made.

    B. In 1951 the British tried but failed.

    C. In 1952 the Swiss paved the way for an ascent that would succeed.

IV. The near success of the 1952 Swiss team paved the way for the British

victory.

        A. The Royal Geographical Society and the Alpine
             Club sponsored the event.

        B. Colonel John Hunt, leader of the team, planned
             carefully and thoroughly.

V. The actual ascent was accomplished in steps and presented problems

solvable by team effort only.

        A. Ice falls and crevasses endangered the team.

        B. The team set up a series of base camps at high
             altitudes.

        C. They set up the last camp, by necessity, close
             enough for ascent and descent of the peak in
             one day.

VI. Finally, Hillary and Tenzing began their ascent.

        A. A storm forced a delay.

        B. The day of 29 May 1953 began with a problem,
             but ended with victory.

        C. Hillary, an Englishman, and Tenzing, a Sherpa,
             had completed the conquest of Everest.

Conclusion: Hillary and Tenzing did not humble Everest alone. They stood

on the summit with hundreds of teammates.

112

In the Himalayas, a mountain range that separates Tibet and Nepal, is located the tallest mountain on earth. The Tibetans refer to it as Chomolungma. Scholars translate that name to "Goddess Mother of the World." The Sherpa people call it "Mountain-So-High-No-Bird-Can-Fly-Over-It."[1] In 1849, the Surveyor General of India, Sir George Everest, designated the mountain as Peak XV. He entered no special notation while recording his findings taken from a vantage point in India and using scientific instruments. It was three years later before his calculations translated into feet above sea level. He determined that Peak XV was 29,002 feet high. Sir George's findings were checked from six different points and declared correct. Peak XV received a new name, Mount Everest, in honor of its discoverer.[2] In 1953, Edmund Hillary and Norgay Tenzing ascended Mount Everest and became the first men to stand on its summit. They did not accomplish this feat alone, for Everest was not subdued by the two men who reached its summit on 29 May 1953, but over a period of thirty-two years and by hundreds of men.

Although it was determined in 1852 that Everest was the tallest mountain on earth, the impulse to scale its heights was restrained because of superstition and misinformation. Its location was remote. The governments of both Tibet and Nepal distrusted outsiders, and the inhabitants of these two countries were exceedingly superstitious. There seemed to be no way anyone

---

[1] Ann Terry White, _All About Mountains and Mountaineering_ (New York: Random House, 1962), pp. 112-113.

[2] Leonard Wibberley, _The Epics of Everest_ (Garden City, N.Y.: Country Life Press, 1954), p. 2.

from without or within would ascend the mountain. Early nineteenth century
cartographers completely ignored mapping of the area because "geographers
didn't know which peak was which or how high any of them were."[3] Despite
the mountain's remoteness and ignorance of its topography, interest in the
mountain continued.

Eventually, Tibet opened the way for Europeans to explore Mount Everest.
On 9 December 1920, the government of Tibet gave permission for the first
European attempt to scale the mountain.[4] That expedition began in 1921 and
ended in disaster. The Europeans, who happened to be British, lacked the
necessary experience for climbing in the Himalayas. As sea level people,
they were not acclimated to the high altitudes. Many died or became ill.[5]
The second reconnaissance occurred in 1922. Learning from the previous
failure, this British group improved their plans. They employed Sherpas
to assist in their ascent.[6] The Sherpas had physical differences which
enabled them to be vigorous in high altitudes. They had twenty percent
more blood. With this increased volume and, consequently, more red corpuscles, Sherpas' blood caught more oxygen and absorbed it into their systems.

---

[3] White, _All About Mountains_, p. 111.

[4] Sir John Hunt, "Triumph on Everest," _The National Geographic Magazine_,
106 (July 1954), 2.

[5] "Mount Everest," _Encyclopaedia Britannica_ (1973), VIII, 900.

[6] Sherpas are a race of people, Tibetan in origin, who inhabit the
southern flanks of the Himalayan Mountains. They are loyal and cour-
ageous, according to Sir Edmund Hillary, writing in the preface of his
book, _Schoolhouse in the Clouds_ (Garden City, N.Y.: Doubleday and
Company, 1964). They are also affectionate and seem unimpressed by
their remarkable toughness.

2

Their blood was thicker and their hearts pumped harder. Their hearts, one-fifth larger than the lowlanders' hearts, beat more slowly. In addition to these blood differences, their respiratory systems empowered their lungs to seize all the oxygen in the air they breathed. More alveoli--small air sacs-- in their large, barrel-shaped lungs made this possible.[7] The added energy enabled the Sherpas to perform the tasks of porter and setting up camps-- especially the high altitude camps--to be chief cook and bottle washers, and to undertake any other jobs that needed to be done. Sherpas did not mind doing the hard chores because they had the physical capabilities and felt a part of the team.[8] The British hoped to ascend the mountain before the southwest monsoon came in early June and deposited heavy snowfalls. The brief, calm period preceding the monsoon passed quickly. The team was slow; the monsoon struck; on 7 June 1922, an avalanche killed seven Sherpas, ending the attempt.[9] During the next twenty or so years, other attempts ended in failure. After the 1922 efforts, on 6 June 1924, George Leigh Mallory and Andrew Irvine started for the summit using "English Air."[10] They vanished from sight just eight hundred feet from the peak. George Mallory's obsession was "to string her very nose tip." It was the third Everest attempt he had been a part of. "We expect no mercy from Everest," he had said. He received none. For nine years Everest remained undisturbed. Then, in 1933,

----

[7] Lorus Milne, Jr., and Margery Milne, The Mountains (New York: Time, 1962), pp. 121-132.

[8] White, All About Mountains, pp. 116-117.

[9] Britannica, pp. 900-901.

[10] "The Conquest of Everest," Life, 29 June 1953, p. 18. "English Air" is what the Sherpas called oxygen tanks. Some Everesters rejected them as un-sporting.

[11] Ibid.

3

F. S. Smythe and Eric E. Shipton found George Mallory's ice axe sixty feet below the crest of the northeast ridge. High winds stopped their team's endeavors.[12] In 1934, Maurice Wilson died while climbing alone. His body and diary were recovered by the 1935 team that also failed, as did the 1936 and 1938 teams.[13]

Then came World War II. The Chinese invaded Tibet during the war and closed the northern route.[14] This route had always been used because the southern aspect of Everest was considered unclimbable.[15] Although the Nepalese government opened its route toward the southern exposure, it would allow only one nation each year to attempt the ascent.[16] The restrictions on the nations and adverse climatic conditions did not encourage climbers. The hot weather in India and the cool Tibetan weather cause the peaks of Everest to be battered by fierce storms. Just a few weeks in the spring and the early fall are suitable for climbing. This short time period added pressure to the teams exploring an unfamiliar route. In 1951, a deep crevasse forced a British team to detour. In 1952, the youngest member of a Swiss team was lowered sixty feet to a shelf in the crevasse. He then crossed over to the other wall of the opening and climbed up on the other side. The other

---

[12] _Britannica_, p. 901.

[13] _Ibid._

[14] Hunt, National _Geographic_, p. 4.

[15] _Ibid._, p. 17.

[16] White, _All About Mountains_, p. 122.

4

mountaineers threw ropes across to him and made a rope ladder.[17] The Swiss

tried twice in 1952. Both times they failed; however, two of the men on the

team, Raymond Lambert and Norgay Tenzing, pushed up to 28,000 feet on 27 May,

higher than anyone before them had ever climbed.[18]

The near success of the 1952 Swiss team paved the way for the British

victory. The British were sponsored by the Royal Geographical Society and

the Alpine Club. John Hunt, the leader of the team, had been a snow-warfare

instructor. Using his experience, he trained the other twelve members on the

steep Scotland tors and in the Alps.[19] Hunt required his climbers to be

between twenty-five and forty years old and to have had Himalayan climbing

experience. In addition to thoroughly training the men, John Hunt planned

every step. Before the climbers arrived on the scene, he assembled equipment

and mobilized a brigade of porters to carry the "tons of supplies from Bombay

to Katmandu." The 450 carriers packed the load seventeen days, over 175 miles,

to reach Thyangboche. Everest was still fifteen miles away.[20] The porters

were paid three rupees--sixty-three cents--a day to carry a forty pound load,

consisting of tents, food, kerosene, candles, matches, and oxygen bottles.

It was the best, warmest, most nourishing, strongest, and lightest food and

equipment that British science could devise. The porters went through passes

[17] *Ibid.*, p. 125.

[18] *Britannica*, p. 902.

[19] *Life*, p. 25.

[20] Hunt, *National Geographic*, p. 5.

10,000 feet high, and down in hot, humid valleys only 4,000 feet above sea level. After the climbers assembled, they trained for three weeks on neighboring peaks of the Himalayan range. This period spent by the climbers in training gave their bodies time to adapt. Their bone marrow count changed from its sea-level five million red corpuscles per cubic millimeter to eight million. Their heart and lung muscles adjusted.[21] Climbers chose their favorite foods to pack in. Men lose several pounds each day when working at altitudes of 20,000 feet. Their liquid intake is five or more pints greater per day at high altitudes. The climbers considered all of these facts when the food was brought into Base Camp I near the foot of the Khumbu ice fall.

The actual ascent was accomplished in steps, each presenting problems, solvable by team effort only. The ice fall at Base Camp I had crevasses, often concealed by snow, throughout. Pillars of ice tumbled without warning, and sunlight sent rays of light, blinding the men and bringing heat. The porters' uneasiness in Base Camp I was not much relieved in the next camp, located in the middle of the ice fall. Camp III, situated at the top of the slowly moving ice fall, caused constant anxiety for everyone present.[22] Camp III, at 20,200 feet, measured just one hundred feet less than Mount McKinley, North America's highest peak, and just one-third of the distance to Everest Peak. Camps IV and V, located in the Western Cwm,[23] ranged in

  ----

  [21]
  Hunt, National Geographic, p. 8.
  [22]
  Wibberley, Epics, pp. 208-209.
  [23]
  A "cwm" is a Welsh word, pronounced "coom," meaning enclosed valley.
Cwms are usually found on a mountain's flank.

altitudes from 21,200 feet to 24,000 feet. On lower Lhotse, Everest's

neighboring peak, Camps VI and VII were at 23,000 and 24,000 feet. At

25,800 feet, in the South Col,[24] Hunt, Bourdillon, and Evans set up Camp

VIII. They were assisted by nineteen Sherpas who packed in five hundred

pounds of supplies. Six of the Sherpas traveled back and forth twice from

Camp IV. From this vantage point, they effected the supreme effort. Colonel

John Hunt's firm conviction was "that by striving one for all and all for

one" they might "prevail, and then only if Everest gave them the luck of

the weather."[25] The strongest climbers were spared any extra burden so

that they might save their strength. They set up the last camp, by necessity,

close enough for ascent and descent of the peak in one day. Tom Bourdillon

and R. C. Evans tried first. They faltered within three hundred feet of the

summit, higher than any climber before them. They gave Hillary and Tenzing

a minute description of the true summit that had never been seen before. The

Southeast Ridge hid it from view.

Finally, Hillary and Tenzing began their ascent using the new open circuit

oxygen tanks, unlike the closed circuit ones used by Bourdillon and Evans. On 27

and 28 May, they spent two extra days and nights in Camp VIII because of a bad

storm. On 28 May, a support party established Camp IX and left Hillary and Tenz-

ing to spend the night alone.[26] The day of 29 May 1953 began with a problem, but

ended with victory. Hilary had taken off his boots to sleep, and during the

---

[24] A "col" is a depression or a pass in a mountain chain.

[25] *Life*, p. 20.

[26] Milne, *Mountains*, p. 165.

night they froze. Upset, he questioned, "Will we fail because I took off my
boots?"[27] Over a stove, he worked with the leather foot gear for one hour
and eventually got them on. Tenzing and Hillary each wore three pairs of
gloves, made of silk and wool, and windproof. Tenzing wore a red scarf, a
gift from Raymond Lambert, the man who had almost made it to the summit with
him in 1952. They left the tent at 6:00 a.m. In five and one-half torturous
hours they climbed less than four hundred feet. On top, they stood for a
moment then shook hands. But that was not enough for Tenzing, a Sherpa.
He threw his arms around Hillary. They stood thumping each other on the
back until they were almost breathless. Turning off their oxygen, they
looked below at all the peaks. Tenzing unwound four flags--those of the
United Nations, Great Britain, Nepal, and India. Hillary snapped pictures,
and Tenzing buried a packet of candy and the stub of a red and blue pencil,
given to him by his daughter. Silently he prayed, then "covered these
offerings to Chomolungma."[28]

After fifteen minutes on top, they prepared for their descent. Edmund
Hillary, thirty-three years old, a six foot three beekeeper from New Zealand,
had been with only one other Everest team. Norgay Tenzing, thirty-nine years
old, was a Sherpa from Nepal and only five feet three inches tall. He had
been with six teams on the slopes of Everest. They left the summit,
triumphant over a mountain that had been unclimbable for thirty-two years. It
claimed the lives of sixteen men of European origin. More Sherpas had given

---

[27]
  White, _All_ _About_ _Mountains_, p. 130.
[28]
  Ibid., pp. 134-135.

their lives than had people from all the other nations added together. Surely,
it is evident that Hillary and Tenzing did not humble Everest alone. They
stood on the summit with hundreds of teammates.

9

Bibliography

"Conquest of Everest, The." Life, 34 (29 June 1953), 18-25.

"Everest, Mount." Encyclopaedia Britannica. 20 vols. (1973), VIII, 900-903.

Hillary, Sir Edmund. Schoolhouse in the Clouds. Garden City, N.Y.:
    Doubleday and Company, 1964.

Hunt, Sir John. "Triumph on Everest." The National Geographic
    Magazine, 106 (July 1954), 1-64.

Milne, Lorus, Jr., and Margery Milne. The Mountains. New York:
    Time, 1962.

White, Anne Terry. All About Mountains and Mountaineering. New York:
    Random House, 1962.

Wibberley, Leonard. The Epics of Everest. Garden City, N.Y.:
    Country Life Press, 1954.

10

The following questions on "The Humbling of Everest" will provide you with a thorough review of the elements of a research paper. You should now be able to answer these questions. If you cannot, review the sections of the text dealing with your area of weakness.

Content

1. Where are the title of the paper, the student's name, and the date placed?

2. What information is included in the first paragraph?

3. What is the thesis of the paper? Copy the thesis sentence here.

4. Where is the thesis sentence located in the paper?

5. What sequence is used to organize the ideas and events discussed in the paper?

6. List here the sentences that begin the six major divisions of the paper.

    a.

    b.

    c.

    d.

    e.

    f.

7. What is the conclusion of the paper?

Outline

1.(a) Where is the thesis statement placed?

(b) What is its function? Its relationship to the rest of the outline?

2.(a) How are the major divisions of the outline indicated?

(b) What is the function of each of these major divisions?

3. How are supporting materials for each of the major divisions indicated?

4. How many divisions are required to support each major division?

5. What procedures can be used to check an outline to determine whether or not it will fulfill its function?

6. What grammatical form does every item in this outline take?

Documentation Forms

1. How is material to be footnoted indicated *in the text?*

2. What kinds of information must have a footnote?

3. How are footnotes numbered, indented, spaced, and punctuated?

4.(a) See footnote 1. Copy the information as it is given.

(b) In what footnote is this book cited next? Copy the information in this footnote.

(c) How does it differ from footnote 1?

(d) How many times is the book referred to in footnote citations? In how many different forms?

5.(a) See footnote 4. Copy the information as it is given.

(b) In what footnote is this magazine article referred to next? Copy the footnote. How does it differ from footnote 4?

6.(a) See footnote 5. Copy the information exactly as it is given.

(b) In what footnote is this source referred to next? Copy it here. How does it differ from the first citation?

7.(a) See footnote 10. Copy the information exactly as it is given.

(b) In what footnote is this source referred to next? How does this second citation differ from the first? Where is the next citation? How does it differ from the first?

8. See footnotes 6, 10, 23, and 24. What materials do these footnotes contain? How do they differ from other footnotes?

Bibliography

1. What determines the order of the individual entries?

2. How are the entries indented?

3. Examine the first entry. List the information in the order given; label each item.

a.

b.

c.

d.

e.

What marks of punctuation are used to separate and identify each item?

4. Examine the second entry. Why is the volume number given in Roman numerals and the pages in Arabic numbers?

5.(a) Examine the third entry. List the information in the order given: label each item.

      a.

      b.

      c.

      d.

      e.

(b) What marks of punctuation are used to separate and identify items?

(c) Why is the author's name inverted?

6.(a) Examine the fourth entry. List the information in the order given; label each item.

      a.

      b.

      c.

      d.

      e.

      f.

(b) How does this entry differ from the first entry?

7. How do bibliographical entries differ from footnote entries as to:
   a. Author's name.

   b. Punctuation: for books.

                      for magazines.

   c. Page numbers: for books.

                      for magazines.

   d. Indentation and spacing.

Assignment:
Third Research Paper

You have been introduced to and have practiced locating appropriate materials in the library, taking notes, narrowing the subject, formulating a thesis sentence and from it developing an outline, writing the paper, documenting with footnotes, and listing all sources in a bibliography. You have written two research papers according to certain limitations and specifications. This third assignment will allow for more flexibility should your instructor and you so desire. For any successful paper, however, you do need to choose a subject and have some notion of length. Where variations in form are possible, you must know which ones your instructor will accept or which ones you choose to use. Therefore, a specification (instruction) form is included for you to complete. You will also find several topics and kinds of research papers suggested. Unless your instructor indicates a subject preference, read all the options; decide which one appeals to you and select the subject you prefer.

PLAN SHEET

Subject: _____

Length: _____

Requirements:

    1. _____

    2. _____

    3. _____

    4. _____

Completed paper must include:

1. _____

2. _____

3. _____

4. _____

5. _____

6. _____

Schedule:

Subject chosen: _____

Bibliography cards and note cards checked: _____

Thesis and sentence outline checked: _____

Paper due: _____

OPTION "A"

All the world loves a mystery! For centuries the great mysteries of the world have driven men and women to seek explanations and offer solutions to them. Still the mysteries remain, and still men search to explain them. In reality, perhaps men do not love mysteries as much as they hate unanswered questions.

These mysteries, myths, wonders, and unknowns are among those still perplexing human beings. Select one topic of the following:

1. What Indians built Mesa Verde? When? Why did they leave?

2. What are some explanations for the occurrence of pyramids both in Egypt and in Central America?

3. Why did the Aztecs let Cortez into their lands? When did they receive their ideas of a white god who would one day return?

4. What are some of the legends surrounding Quetzalcoatl? What was his relationship to the Aztecs, Mayans, and Toltecs?

5. Was Atlantis real or just a product of Plato's imagination?

6. Who built Stonehenge? When? Why?

7. Who created the huge stone statues on Easter Island? What is their significance?

8. What are some of the legends and myths connected with sea monsters? Are there any realistic explanations for their existence?

9. What are some of the legends associated with the Holy Grail? Is it real? Or does it exist only in legends?

10. When and where were the Dead Sea Scrolls discovered? What new light on biblical history do they shed?

11. Why were the Egyptian pyramids built? What puzzles about them remain unsolved?

12. Why was the discovery of Tutankhamen's Tomb an archeological wonder? What did archeologists learn from it?

13. What was Heinrich Schliemann's greatest achievement? What obstacles did he have to overcome?

14. Do "the canals on Mars" exist? What explanations are offered for them? What are the latest findings about them?

15. Are there now, or have there ever been, human vampires? Where did the vampire legends begin? What are some of the legends?

16. What is known of "the lost city of Machu Picchu"? What is still unknown about the city?

17. What has been the history of the Hope Diamond? What are some of the mysteries surrounding it?

18. What are some of the myths and the unknowns connected with the sinking of the *Titanic* on April 15, 1912?

19. What are some of the legends and unknowns about the assassination of President Lincoln?

20. What is known about the disappearance of Amelia Earhart? What is unknown?

OPTION "B"

If Horace Greeley were alive today, the pressure of the equal rights groups might cause him to revise his famous statement, "Go West, young man, go West," to "Go West, young person, go West." Regardless of the gender of the statement, the advice is still sound, for the Western United States offers a wealth of material suitable for research topics.

"This assignment, should you decide to accept it," will allow you to choose a topic ranging from the plentiful historical sagas of how the West was won to the unique social systems created by freeways, oil spills, and Disneyland.

Subject: The Western United States. (This is the broad, general topic.)

You must narrow your topic to one person, place, event, or

problem specifically related to the West. The topic may focus on the past, present, or future of the West.

OPTION "C"

When you were a child, you often played "make-believe." Wearing an astronaut's headgear, you guided Apollo XII to the moon; from the branches of the backyard apple tree as Tarzan or Jane, you became lord of the jungle; from a plastic doctor's or nurse's kit, you administered shots and prescribed medication for your neighborhood friends; on the patio, you set up housekeeping and made frequent trips to the refrigerator-market to feed an assemblage of doll and kitten children. You were role playing, a process that psychiatrists say enables the individual to better comprehend and understand the problems of others.

Certainly, if you walk for a while in the shoes of another, you can more fully empathize with him. An understanding of the life and times of someone in the past provides a foundation upon which to build the present. For this assignment you are to become a person living at a particular time in the past. Write your paper in the third person, *not* first person. You might choose to be:

A woman leaving the relative security of the Virginia colony, crossing the Appalachians to settle with her family in Kentucky.

A laborer working to build an Egyptian pyramid.

A young Indian boy about to be initiated into the tribe.

A young black man crossing the Atlantic in a slave ship to be sold in the Carolinas.

Henry VIII deciding to break with the Catholic Church to establish the Church of England.

Marie Antoinette on the day before she is executed.

John Wilkes Booth deciding to assassinate President Lincoln.

A young person working in a factory in Dickens' London.

A young militia man fighting at Lexington.

A young woman struggling to become a doctor in the late nineteenth century.

Father Kino establishing missions throughout the Southwest.

Harriet Tubman smuggling slaves to the North.

Choose your own role and your particular moment in history. Of course, you will have to become thoroughly familiar with the times. You will have to get "inside the skin" of the person you become.

After thoroughly researching the lives of Wilbur and Orville Wright and the first flight of a powered aeroplane on 17 December 1903, one student, intrigued with the idea of what a photographer would have recorded that day, assigned himself the role of a U.S. Coast Guard cameraman. The following paragraphs begin his story:

On the 17th of December in 1903 a most important event took place that was to sway the aviation history of the entire world. Although few people witnessed the incident, soon the whole world was to share in the excitement. As a cameraman for the U.S. Coast Guard at Kitty Hawk, North Carolina, John T. Daniels was assigned to cover the astonishing news being made as Orville and Wilbur Wright successfully flew a powered aeroplane.

It was a bitterly cold December morning, and, as John Daniels rose from bed and peered out the foggy window, he could see Captain A. D. Estheridge struggling his way through the strong wind to reach the bunkhouse. Daniels finished dressing and pulled on his boots. Estheridge entered the bunkhouse and told Daniels that the two of them were to cover the trials at the Kill Devil sandhills. Daniels asked, "What trials?" Estheridge laughed, saying, "Two eccentric brothers, who think man was meant to fly, are going to try to fly a powered aeroplane." As Estheridge took Daniels' coat from the locker and handed it to him, Daniels got out his camera, tripod, and film so he could take pictures of the "eccentric brothers" and the stunts they were going to perform.

Mervin Dobson

OPTION "D"

Alvin Toffler, in his best seller, *Future Shock*, concerned that the rapid rate of change was causing stress and sickness among thousands who found it shattering to cope with such change, suggested looking the future squarely in the eye. He proposed that whereas historians have studied the past to become acquainted with the present, it might be time to turn our vision to the future to gain valuable insights into the present. This exercise of "future exploration" can be helpful in increasing "future consciousness" and perhaps can help us to become more successful in coping with it.

This option requires you to explore, create, forecast, and perhaps prophesy the design of life style in the year 2000. You need not be frightened to speak with certainty for you, like the scientist, will be relying upon evidence, impressions, and opinions, of well-known people. You will be applying deductive reasoning to arrive at conclusions. You need not worry about being right—for that type of judgment need not apply. You should, however, strive for logical possibilities.

You might pursue any of the following:

The kitchen of the future

The educational system (any level)

Communications: mail, radio, television, etc.

Transportation, i.e., the status of the private automobile

Political party systems

Individual life styles

Professional and amateur sports

Parent-child relationships

The monetary system

Supermarket designs

The art world

Military structures

Energy sources and uses

Suggestion: In researching this area, several subject headings may be helpful. The *Reader's Guide* uses "future," "futurism," and "forecasting" as headings. Follow suggested cross references and "see also" headings as well. In addition, some indexes direct the researcher to specific years, such as "nineteen eighty-four," "two thousand," or "three thousand." Several journals are published which center on futurism.

OPTION "E"

Scholars have advanced intriguing theories concerning the origin of human language. Some suggest that speech developed in imitation of animal or natural sounds; others that pain, anger, or stress forced "oh's" and "ah's" from human lips and that these spontaneous sounds developed into language patterns. All of these suggestions are possibilities, but we do not know now, and probably never will know, exactly when or how man began to speak.

We are not, however, totally ignorant about language behavior. We do know that languages change; we know that words enter a language, are used for a time, and then disappear, or that they enter in one form and with a certain meaning, then through the years change forms and meanings. Studying the history of words is in itself an engrossing task, for the story of words is closely tied to the story of people. The etymology of a word embodies its entire history: when it entered a language; its form(s) and meaning(s) at that time; its development and changes during its years of use; and its present status, as a single word, combined with other words, and used in phrases.

For this assignment, select a word that has been in the English language for at least five hundred years. You can check the word's entrance date into the language in *The Oxford English Dictionary*. Through the use of dictionaries, books devoted to the history of words and to regional differences and dialects, and articles in language publications, assemble information necessary to write a history of the word.

One student chose the word *theatre*. As she progressed in her research, she found that *theatre* had a fascinating history and that a number of words and terms had clustered around the concept of theatre. She finally selected the following stage terms to discuss in her paper: *theatre, scene, proscenium,* coming from the Greek theater; *box office,* from the Latin; *royalty,* from the English; and *angel, Annie Oakley,* and *George Spelvin,* from the American.

The thesis for her paper was as follows: The word *theatre* and several theatrical terms originated in ancient times, whereas other terms have evolved through the centuries.

Here are some paragraphs from her paper:

SAMPLE I

Theatre itself is Greek in origin. The Greek word *théa* meant "sight or view" and *theates* was "a spectator or a person who viewed something." When the first open air coliseum was constructed to house the religious festivals of the Greeks, the construction was called a *theatron,* literally meaning "a place for viewing." It is believed that the form *theatron* came from *theasthai,* "to behold." The Romans were far behind the Greeks in the development of public places for viewing. They termed their outdoor coliseum *theatrum,* and the word came to be used in the vernacular of the Latin speaking peoples. In the twelfth to thirteenth centuries, the old French language developed the form *theatre* or *teatre.* The former French form was used by the English and is the most widely used form of the word today.[2]

SAMPLE II

The special section of the theatre responsible for obtaining an audience to view the performance and performers is the *box office*. The history of this term began with the old theatrical meaning of *box*. The word *box* might have been an independent adoption of the Latin word *buxum,* meaning "boxwood, a type of tree," in the sense of "a thing made from wood or *buxum*."[23] *The Oxford English Dictionary* gives the theatrical meaning of *box* as "a seated compartment in a theatre, at first specially for ladies: private-, front-, side-, etc."[24]

SAMPLE III

That part of the theatre building which sold admission tickets to the exclusive box seats was soon known as the *box office*. The term *box office* has remained to the present day and now is "an office in a theatre, commonly in the outer lobby, where tickets are sold."[26] *Box office,* shortened to B.O. by theatre people, also may be used to "indicate the appeal of a play to the public" or the amount of audience drawing power the play has.[27] An actor may be said to be *good box office* if he is able to draw a large audience. Pertaining to the business side of a theatrical production, *box office receipts* are "the total monies brought in from the performance of a play." A show or performance which does not bring in high receipts or is poorly received by the public is said to be a *box office flop.*

BARBARA YOUNG

Some possible word choices are:

sinister	citizen	color	ring
gossip	king	high	salt
assassin	gold	horse	shade
marshal	humor	house	dragon
villain	blood	meat	coliseum

You have thousands to chose from.

OPTION "F"

Writing a research paper about a literary work should help increase your understanding of and appreciation for a particular novel, drama, short story, or poem. You may write a paper using only the work itself and your perceptions and analyses. A research paper, however, demands that you investigate concerns outside of, but relating to, the literature. After you have decided upon the literary work you wish to write about, read it carefully, then choose one of the following questions as a beginning point for your research. Not all of these questions will apply to all works, but several will apply to any one work.

1. How is this work related to others by the same author? Are the plot, characterizations, setting, theme, and tone similar or dissimilar?

2. How does this work reflect the time when it was written? You may need to limit your research to one area: political, economic, cultural, religious, or ethical.

3. If the work focuses upon a social problem or problems, delineate the problems in real life and the work's treatment of them.

4. How was this work received by the public? By the critics?

5. What element or elements of the work have provoked comment?

6. Does an understanding of the work as a whole or portions of it depend upon understanding the tenets of either a particular religion or a particular philosophy?

7. Does an understanding of the work depend upon understanding beliefs and practices in a particular culture?

8. Is the work based upon folklore or mythology? If so, how does an understanding of the folklore or mythology contribute to a comprehension of the work?

9. Does the work treat an ethnic or racial group unfairly? If so, how?

10. How have interpretations of the work changed through the years?

11. If the work is about a historical person, does it function more as biography or fiction?

One student decided to investigate the life of Thomas More as depicted in Robert Bolt's *A Man for All Seasons* and in historical records. The introduction to her paper was the following:

> The fundamental issue of ethical philosophy is the nature of good conduct. Men have wrestled for centuries with the apparent dichotomy between spiritual and temporal good and between idealistic and realistic motives. If a man has a strong sense of duty to himself, society, and God, he must consider the higher and lower demands of each and reconcile them with his ideals. Those men are fortunate whose duties harmonize. Thomas More was not fortunate. From the time he rose to prominence, he struggled, trying to mediate among his inclinations: his desire to live happily (or, at least, survive), his love for family and friends, his duty to law and society, his duty to his king, and his devotion to God. He did not find a simple solution to the question of good conduct, but one obtains from an account of his experiences, both from historical records and from Robert Bolt's *A Man for All Seasons*, a sense of the conscientious diplomacy required in a man's internal affairs if he is to be called virtuous.
>
> JANENE MCNEIL

This research paper, "The Last Union Soldier," is included to show both topic and sentence outline forms. It shows placement of footnotes at the *end* of the paper instead of at the bottom of each page.

THE LAST UNION SOLDIER

A Term Paper
Submitted in Partial Fulfillment of the
Course Requirements for
English-102
Section 2622

by

Cynthia Linnae
13 March 1976

138

The Last Union Soldier

Thesis: With the death of Albert Woolson, the last soldier of the Union
         Army, on 2 August 1956, an era of American history died.

I.   Albert's life

   A. Birth

   B. Apprenticeship

   C. Father's war service

   D. Family's move

II.   Albert's Civil War days

   A. Enlistment

   B. Service

   C. Discharge

   D. Return to civilian life

III. Albert's life after the war

   A. First marriage

   B. Second marriage

   C. Children

   D. Member of G.A.R.

   E. One hundredth birthday

   F. Death

IV.   Albert's funeral

   A. Last Union veteran

   B. Duluth services

   C. Ritual

   D. Attendance

   E. Final taps

Conclusion: With the death of Mr. Woolson, remembered and honored as the last
             survivor of an age, an era of American history closed.

Thesis: With the death of Albert Woolson, the last soldier of the Union Army, on 2 August 1956, an era of American history died.

I.   Albert Woolson led a quiet, ordinary life from boyhood to manhood.

    A. On a farm in New York state, Woolson was born on 11 February 1847.

    B. Albert became an apprentice, following his father's trade as a carpenter.

    C. Albert and his mother moved to Minnesota after a year of waiting for the elder Woolson's return from the war.

    D. Albert's father was hospitalized in Minnesota after the Battle of Shiloh, with a leg wound.

    E. The Woolson family moved to New Janesville, Minnesota, but shortly after, Albert's father died.

II.   The war days of Albert Woolson were few.

    A. Albert enlisted in the First Minnesota Regiment of Heavy Artillery at the age of seventeen.

    B. Under the command of General George H. Thomas, Albert served as a drummer boy when the Union forces beat Hood's Confederates in the Battle of Nashville.

    C. Albert fired a cannon only once.

    D. Discharged on 7 September 1865, Albert returned to carpentry as a livelihood.

III. After the Civil War, Albert retired to a simple life.

    A. Sarah Jane Sloper became Albert's first wife in 1868, but in 1901 Sarah Jane died.

    B. Albert's second wife was Anna Haugen, whom he married in 1904.

    C. Albert was the father of six daughters and two sons.

    D. In 1950, Woolson became Commander in Chief of the Grand Army of the Republic (G.A.R.).

E. With the death of James A. Hard in 1953, Woolson became the last member of the G.A.R.

F. On Albert Woolson's one hundredth birthday, Harry Truman sent him a telegram.

G. He lived nine more years.

IV. A full-scale funeral was planned for Albert Woolson.

A. Albert was the last of some 2,675,000 Union veterans.

B. The funeral was at the National Guard Armory, at two o'clock in the afternoon, 4 August 1956.

C. One hundred churches tolled their bells at two o'clock in Albert Woolson's honor.

D. Albert Woolson's body was dressed in a blue Union Army uniform.

E. The funeral was attended by three thousand people.

F. At the funeral a good friend said, "Taps are sounded, lights are out, the soldier sleeps."

Conclusion: With the death of Mr. Woolson, remembered and honored as the last survivor of an age, an era of American history closed.

An aged and wrinkled body lay in peaceful silence on a clean sheeted
bed in St. Luke's Hospital of Duluth, Minnesota. The family had tearful
eyes as they remembered how their dear one had entered the hospital with
lung congestion, slipped into a coma, and died without regaining consciousness. The man's death had been inevitable. He had been one hundred
and nine that past February, and with illness and age against him he had
no chance to recover.[1] His passing was not only felt by his family, but by
millions of Americans who witnessed the end of an age. The date was
2 August 1956, when Albert Woolson, the last soldier of the Union Army,
passed away, and with his death an era of American history died too.

Albert Woolson led a quiet, ordinary life from boyhood to manhood.
As an only child, Albert had to mature quickly. He was born on a hamlet
farm on 11 February 1847, in New York state.[2] When he came of age his
father made him his apprentice in the trade of carpentry. A plea from
President Lincoln called more men to war, and, in answer to the cry, Albert's
father left home to join the Union Army. After a year of waiting for some
message concerning Mr. Woolson, Albert and his mother began an extensive
research of Army records. Through these records they found that Albert's
father, severely wounded in the leg, had been last seen at the Battle of Shiloh.
More searching indicated that he had been taken to Duluth, Minnesota, to have

his gangrene-infected leg amputated. Albert and his mother began the long journey from New York to Duluth. After finding their loved one, they relocated in New Janesville, Minnesota, where, shortly after the move, Albert's father died.[3] Albert supported his mother and himself with the skills of carpentry until he turned seventeen. Then he, too, eagerly joined the battle of the States.

The war days that Albert engaged in were few. He enlisted as a drummer for the First Minnesota Heavy Artillery Regiment in October of 1864.[4] Under the command of General George H. Thomas, Albert served as a drummer boy when the Union forces beat Hood's Confederates in the Battle of Nashville.[5] Although he never actually fought in battle, Albert played an important role by encouraging the men onward with his constant rhythm:

> We went along with a burying detail. Going out we played
> proper sad music, but coming back we kinda hit it up. Once
> a woman asked me what kind of music was that to bury some-
> body. I told her that we had taken care of the dead, and
> that we were now cheering up the living.[6]

A favorite quick step that the drummers played as they marched in a precise line was "The Girl I Left Behind Me." Albert said that song seemed to liven up the troops and give them new strength to march forward.[7] Albert fired a cannon only once. The event took place in any army camp, as the war was coming to a close:

"The borned gunners just wanted to hear the noise," Albert stated. "The colonel handed me the end of a rope and said, 'When I yell, you stand on your toes, open your mouth wide, give a yell yourself and pull the rope.' I yanked the lanyard and the cannon went off and scared me half to death."[8]

Discharged on 7 September 1865, Albert returned home to Minnesota to continue as a carpenter.[9]

After the Civil War, Albert retired to a simple life. Three years after his discharge he fell in love with and married Sarah Jane Sloper. In 1901, thirty-three years later, she died. In 1904, Albert took a second wife, Anna Haugen.[10] Albert's family of six daughters and two sons grew up in the village of Windom, Minnesota. In 1950, Albert Woolson was honored by being named Senior Vice Commander-in-Chief of the Grand Army of the Republic (G.A.R.). The G.A.R., composed of the original Union Army members, was once a rightly influential group in the country's politics. With the death of James A. Hard in 1953, Albert became the last member of the G.A.R.[11] When Mr. Woolson reached his nineties he moved to Duluth, Minnesota. During these last years, Albert spent time visiting children at a nearby school where he lectured to them about thrift and gave out a few shiny pennies. In return, the children collected 27,652 pennies and commissioned an oil painting of Albert. It was hung in the City Council Chamber.[12] The one hundredth birthday of Mr. Woolson brought a telegram from President Harry Truman congratulating him on his successful and long life and upon being the last of 2,675,000 Union veterans.[13] In response Albert said, "I am proud to be the rearguard of such a gallant group of men."[14] The telegram also wished him a continued enjoyable life. Albert lived only nine years after he received this memorable message.

A full scale funeral was planned for Albert Woolson. Because Albert Woolson was the last of 2,675,000 Union soldiers, his funeral, held at the National Guard Armory in Duluth on 4 August 1956, effectively eulogized all of the dead.[15] One hundred churches tolled their bells at two o'clock, and, at their sound, people from all over the city were requested to bow for a word of prayer. The body, handsomely arrayed in a traditional blue Union Army uniform, was laid to rest next to his second wife, Anna, at Park Hill Cemetery in Duluth. One hundred and nine guards, each representing one year of his life, accompanied Mr. Woolson on his last journey. The funeral was attended by approximately three thousand people. The procession, four and one-half miles long, included two hundred cars.[16] A longtime friend of Mr. Woolson closed the service by saying, "Taps are sounded, lights are out, the soldier sleeps."[17]

Albert Woolson did no major heroic feats while he served in the Union Army. He had no charismatic personality that people would remember; he was not known for his vast wealth. What Mr. Woolson did have was a long, fruitful life. He was remembered and honored as the last survivor of an age, a time of turmoil and struggle for the rights of men. President Eisenhower also felt grief at the loss of Mr. Woolson and is quoted as saying, "The American people have lost the last personal link with the Union Army. His passing brings sorrow to the hearts of all who cherish the memory of the brave men on both sides of the War Between the States."[18]

-4-

References Cited

1
   "Last Union Army Veteran Dies; Drummer at 17, He Lives to 109,"
New York *Times*, 3 August 1956, Sec. A, p. 1.

2
   "Duluth Lists Plans for Woolson's Rites," New York *Times*,
4 August 1956, Sec. A, p. 15.

3
   "Albert Woolson," *Time*, 61 (23 March 1953), 25.

4
   "Died--Albert Woolson," *Time*, 48 (13 August 1956), 64.

5
   Time, 23 March 1953, p. 25.

6
   New York *Times*, 3 August 1956, p. 19.

7
   "Muffled Roll for the Grand Army," *Life*, 41 (20 August 1956), 19.

8
   New York *Times*, 3 August 1956, p. 19.

9
   Ibid.

10
   Ibid.

11
   Time, 13 August 1956, p. 64.

12
   New York *Times*, 3 August 1956, p. 19.

13
   "Last Survivor of Union Army," *Time*, 63 (22 February 1954), 48.

14
   Time, 23 March 1953, p. 25.

15
   New York *Times*, 4 August 1956, p. 15.

16
   "Woolson, Last Union Veteran Is Buried After Military Rites,"
New York *Times*, 5 August 1956, Sec. A, p. 76.

17
   Life, 20 August 1956, p. 25.

18
   New York *Times*, 3 August 1956, p. 19.

Bibliography

"Albert Woolson." _Time_, 61 (23 March 1953), 25.

"Died – Albert Woolson." _Time_, 48 (13 August 1956), 64.

"Duluth Lists Plans for Woolson's Rites." New York _Times_,
    4 August 1956, Sec. A, p. 15.

"Last Survivor of Union Army." _Time_, 63 (22 February 1954), 48.

"Last Union Army Veteran Dies; Drummer at 17, He Lives to 109."
    New York _Times_, 3 August 1956, Sec. A, pp. 1, 19.

"Memorial to Union Army." New York _Times_, 12 August 1956, Sec. A,
    p. 84.

"Muffled Role for the Grand Army." _Life_, 41 (20 August 1956),
    19-25.

"Woolson, Last Union Veteran Is Buried After Military Rites,"
    New York _Times_, 5 August 1956, Sec. A, p. 76.

-6-

147

Typing

Suggestions for Typing Your Paper

Certain regulations, if they are consistently used throughout your paper, will make the paper more readable.

1. Use standard size 8½ × 11 inch typing paper. All research papers should be typed.

2. Use a title page containing title of paper, your name, and the course name and number for which the paper is written. (A sample is included in this section.)

3. Place the outline page after the title page; place thesis appropriately at the top of the outline page.

4. Double space when typing. This is not only for neatness: it will leave space for comments and corrections.

5. Leave reasonable margins of at least one inch around the paper. A margin of one and one-half inches on the left side is often used to allow space for securing the paper into a binder without interfering with print.

6. Indent paragraphs, footnotes, and the second line of bibliographies five spaces.

7. Number pages in Arabic numerals either in the upper right-hand corner, the middle of the lower margin, or the middle of the upper margin. Be consistent.

Inserting a sample page with these margins in your typewriter underneath your sheet will enable you to set up the page with appropriate spacing of margins and footnotes.

Note the placement of the following:

1. Page number may appear in the upper right corner or in the middle top or bottom of the page. In the upper right corner, the number should be one-half inch from the top at the right margin.

2. Widths of margins are shown one and one-half inches at top, one and one-half inches on the left margin, one inch on the right margin, and one inch on the bottom margin.

3. The text of the paper continues to the "last line of text" leaving two spaces or about one-half inch between the last line and the dividing line for footnotes.

4. **The dividing line is fifteen underscores or about one and one-half inches in length. Drop down two more spaces and begin footnotes.**

5. Footnotes are indented as you indent a paragraph, single-spaced within the citation if more than one line is needed, and double-spaced between **footnotes.**

Last line of text.

———————————

[1]
Footnote xxxxxxxxxxxxxxxxxxxxxxxxxxxxxxxxxxxxxxxxxxxxxxxxxxxxxx
xxxxxxxxxxxxxxxxxxxxxxxxxxx.

[2]
Footnote xxxxxxxxxxxxxxxxxxxxxxxxxxxxxxxxxxxxxxxxxxxxxxxxxxxxxx
xxxxxxxxxxxxxxxxxxxxxxxxxxx.

[3]
Footnote xxxxxxxxxxxxxxxxxxxxxxxxxxxxxxxxxxxxxxxxxxxxxxxxxxxxxx
xxxxxxxxxxxxxxxxxxxxxxxxxxx.

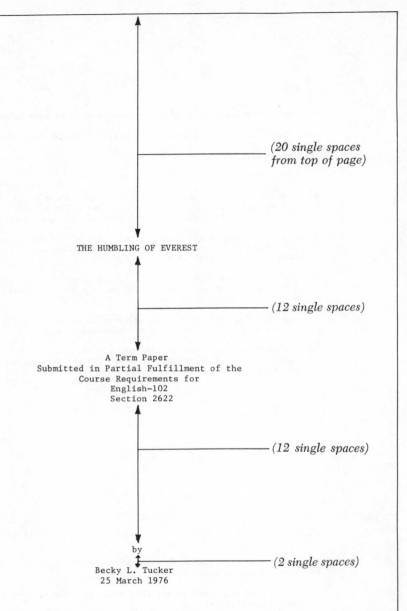

THE HUMBLING OF EVEREST

(20 single spaces from top of page)

(12 single spaces)

A Term Paper
Submitted in Partial Fulfillment of the
Course Requirements for
English-102
Section 2622

(12 single spaces)

by
Becky L. Tucker
25 March 1976

(2 single spaces)

(Well-proportioned, neatly typed pages add to the appeal of your paper. Be consistent in spacing when centering your work, indenting paragraphs, allowing margins, and arranging numbers or lists. This sample page can be used to help space your title page. As the first page your reader will see, it should reflect the neatness and orderliness that lie within.)

8. Elevate footnote numbers at the end of the quoted or paraphrased material. Do not use periods or parentheses after footnote numbers.

9. Type footnotes at the bottom of the page on which the note appears or on a separate page at the end of the paper. Indent the first line of each note five spaces.

10. Single space each footnote and double space between footnotes.

11. Footnotes placed at the end of the paper should be headed "References Cited" or "Endnotes." The format should follow the same rules and arrangement as bottom of the page footnotes, including raised numerals.

12. Proofread VERY CAREFULLY. *You* are responsible for typing errors and careless omissions, not the typist. It is better to write in minor corrections than to leave them uncorrected. If the error is a major one, retype the page.

13. The bibliography is the last sheet. It should be titled "Bibliography." Single space each entry; double space between entries. Indent second and third lines five spaces.

Remember, appearance counts. While your paper may be a masterpiece in content, a poor appearance may turn away the reader.

ABBREVIATIONS

The beginning researcher should avoid extensive use of abbreviations. There is less possibility of error or misunderstanding if words and terms are written in full. Careless abbreviation of words interferes with understanding. While research writing has traditionally utilized abbreviations, the tendency to abbreviate is diminishing. The scholarly Latin words are seldom used, since clear English substitutes serve as well. This list of commonly used abbreviations may prove helpful in reading research material or writing documentation. Use them sparingly. Remember that foreign words and phrases, italicized by printers in professional works, must be underscored in a typed or handwritten paper. Carefully record periods after abbreviations and capitalize as indicated.

ABBREVIATION	MEANING
A.D. = *Anno Domini*	in the year of our Lord (A.D. precedes numerals: A.D. 1960)
anon.	anonymous
B.C.	before Christ (B.C. follows numerals: 600 B.C.)
b.	born
biblio.	bibliography, bibliographer
c.	copyright
c., ca. = *circa*	about (used with approximate dates: ca. 1970)
ch., chs.	chapter, chapters

col., cols.	column, columns
comp.	compiled, compiled by
d.	died
e.g. = *exempli gratia*	for example
et al. = *et alii*	and others (used for more than two authors)
etc. = *et cetera*	and so forth (avoid using)
et seq. = *et sequens*	and the following
fig., figs.	figure, figures
Ibid. = *ibidem*	in the same place (used only in footnotes, always capitalized, because it is the first word, underscored, and followed by a period)
i.e. = *id est*	that is
illus.	illustrated by
introd.	introduction by
loc. cit. = *loco citato*	in the place cited (used in the text to refer to a previous passage)
n.d.	no date of publication
no., nos.	number, numbers
n.p.	no place of publication or no publisher
op. cit. = *opere citato*	in the work cited (used in footnotes only and appears after a name)
p., pp.	page, pages
rev.	review, reviewed by, revision, revised by
rpt.	reprint, reprinted
sic	thus, so (placed in square brackets within quoted material to indicate an obvious error existed in the source: [sic])
trans.	translator, translation, translated by
v., vid. = *vide*	see
vol., vols.	volume, volumes (as used with Arabic numerals as in 3 vols)
Vol., Vols.	Volume, Volumes (as used with Roman numerals as in Vol. III)

Evaluation

Evaluation of Research Paper

Student _____

		Yes	No
Title Page	1. Present		
	2. Done properly		
Thesis Statement	1. Well worded		
	2. Establishes your purpose clearly		
	3. Properly limited		
Outline	1. Contains clear, complete sentences		
	2. Properly set up in two-step format		
	3. Items I, II, and III support the thesis		
Bibliography	1. Alphabetized		
	2. Indented properly		
	3. Books identified properly		
	4. Magazines identified properly		
	5. All information contained in citation		
	6. Citation properly set up		
	7. Consistent form used for all citations		

			Yes	No
Footnotes	1. Numbers properly elevated			
	2. Numerically arranged			
	3. Indented correctly			
	4. Correct placement of footnotes at bottom of page			
	5. Author's name in proper order			
	6. All information properly arranged			
	7. In-text documentation present			
Note Cards	1. Included and arranged in order			
	2. Properly done			

		Excellent	Good	Fair	Poor	None	GRADE:
Writing Skills	1. Introduction						Content ___
	2. Conclusion						Research ___
	3. Text in general						Mechanics ___
	4. Handling of quotations						
	5. Research material						

		Excellent	Good	Fair	Poor
Mechanics	1. Punctuation				
	2. Spelling				
	3. Paragraphing				
	4. Word choice				

General Comments:

Index